PRACTICAL PREPPING:

NO APOCALYPSE REQUIRED

An Everyday Approach to
Disaster Preparedness: Book One

By Steven Konkoly and Randall S. Powers

Copyright Information

Dedication

From Steven

To my wife and children. The reasons I write.

From Randy

For Alice ~ the greatest gift of my life, my partner and my best friend. You hung the moon, and the very stars pale in comparison to your light. Thank you for sharing this human experience with me.

To my parents, Randall and Betty Powers ~ thank you for everything. Your love and support have launched a lifetime of dreams.

To my brother, Joe Powers ~ I am overwhelmed when I think of the man you have become. A loving and dutiful father, husband and son, thank you for living the example.

Acknowledgements

From Steven

To Randy Powers, a good friend and an invaluable member of my beta reading crew. Inviting Randy to co-write this book felt as natural as shaking his hand.

To the thousands of readers that have made *The Jakarta Pandemic* and *The Perseid Collapse Series* a success. Thank you!

From Randy

To my wife, Alice. I could only read over these essays in the middle of the night so many times before my recognition capabilities would simply give up the ghost. Thankfully, I she was always there in the morning to clean things up as my diligent proof reader and *point of view* editor. The overall feel of my portion of this book is truly a blending of our perspectives and I'm just fine with that.

To the production crew that turns the nuts and bolts, I will simply say thank you for all you do. I've worked with a couple of you before on the QSG and I know we are good hands. Steve trusts you completely and I am honored just to step up to the varsity team.

Finally, to our partners, clients and everyone that has been involved in the initiative that is Practical Tactical. THANK YOU for believing in an idea that has become a purpose. We are evolving every day and every discussion, comment and experience has helped shape us and the process of how we operate. Your handprints are all over what we are and that is exactly how we feel it should be.

About Steven Konkoly

Steven Konkoly graduated from the United States Naval Academy and served as a naval officer for eight years in various roles within the Navy and Marine Corps before taking up writing.

His first novel, The Jakarta Pandemic (2010), explored the world of "prepping," well before television and books popularized the concept. Hailed as a "grippingly realistic" family survival story, The Jakarta Pandemic introduced thousands of readers to the unfamiliar concept of "survival in the suburbs," motivating many of them to take the first steps to better prepare themselves for a major disaster. His recently launched series, The Perseid Collapse, continues Steven's legacy of engaging (and informative) post-apocalyptic (SHTF) fiction.

He is the author of critically acclaimed the Black Flagged series: Black Flagged (2011), Black Flagged Redux (2012), Black Flagged Apex (2012) and Black Flagged Vektor (2013). The Perseid Collapse (2013), book one in The Perseid Collapse Series, signaled his return to the post-apocalyptic genre, followed shortly by Event Horizon (2014) and Point of Crisis (2014).

Steven lives with his family in coastal, southern Maine, where he wakes up at "zero dark thirty" to write for most of the day. When "off duty," he struggles to strike a balance between a woefully short sailing season and unreasonably long winter.

Please visit Steven's blog for updates and information regarding all his works:

StevenKonkoly.com

About Randall S. Powers

Randall S. Powers graduated from the Grady College of Journalism and the University of Georgia, building a career in journalism spanning twenty years across all forms of media, including radio, print, digital and television. Since 1998, Randall has worked with an international broadcast media outlet with credits as a media manager, editor, producer, speaker and trainer and has been a contributor on three projects that were awarded the prestigious Peabody Award.

Using the skills gained during his career as a journalist, Randall widened his focus to include disaster preparedness becoming an entrepreneur as the founder and Chief Managing Partner of Practical Tactical, a personal preparedness consulting firm. From this new platform, Randall works as a personal preparedness consultant, public speaker and author.

In 2014, Randall published the Practical Tactical Quick Start Guide as a personal preparedness resource and reference manual designed to help those new to "prepping" develop a well rounded and complete disaster plan without becoming overwhelmed by the process.

Originally from Toccoa, Georgia, Randall lives with his family on their homestead outside of Athens and Atlanta.

Contact Randall directly by email at:
practicaltactical4you@gmail.com or through his website at:

PracticalTactical4you.com

About Practical Prepping: No Apocalypse Required

I'm probably going to overcomplicate things momentarily, but I feel a burning need to explain how *Practical Prepping* is structured. Each chapter starts with a short, related excerpt from one of my books, and is immediately followed by two essays exploring the chapter subject—one by each of the authors.

Why two essays on the same topic? Randy and I share the same preparedness philosophy, but our approach and delivery is different, giving you a richer look at the subject. Also, if you fall asleep reading mine, you can shake it off and give Randy's a try. I can't imagine you'd nod off during one of Randy's essays (hint: he knows way more than I do), so I won't even suggest that the reverse might happen. As a further safeguard, we've taken another step to keep you engaged. Since neither of us wants to inflict a painful lecture on the reader (I start yawning at the thought of a lecture), we agreed to keep the essays light, upbeat and appropriately humorous. Fair warning. I tend to run into trouble with my humor.

Disclaimer: This is not a "HOW TO" manual or a "Survival manifesto." Sure, you'll find some useful lists and a number of highlighted suggestions, but the bulk of this book focuses on ***practical*** first steps you can take, along with ***tactical*** concepts you can embrace—***without seriously interrupting your life or breaking the bank.*** I think you'll be surprised by the significant progress you can make toward a "more prepared" lifestyle by adopting the ***PRACTICAL PREPPING*** mindset.

Don't forget to check out our Pandemic Primer, which you can find at the end of the book or find in the Table of Contents. With the Ebola virus on the loose, and pandemic fears at an all time high, we felt it was only appropriate to provide a no-nonsense look at how to approach and prepare for a pandemic threat.

Contents

PART 1: INTRODUCTION

Steven

Most of you know me better than you think. Sure, by glancing at the author biography on my website or stalking me on Facebook, you can figure out the basics. Ex-military, former pharmaceutical sales representative, early forties, married with two children (boy and girl). *Starting to sound familiar?* It's also no secret that I live in southern Maine, where I enjoy shooting, sailing, gardening and spending time with family. At this point you're probably wondering—*Alex Fletcher? Wait a minute. Are they one and the same?* Yes—and no. After reading more than a thousand pages about Alex, we're going to embark on a discussion about the differences and similarities, framed around an important discussion about preparedness and survival. Quick note: It doesn't matter if you haven't read my novels. You might miss out on a few references, but there is no super-secret handshake or code embedded in the text of my books. This book is designed for everyone.

For those that have read my books, I can sense some of you groaning. *Prepping—with the Fletchers? Sure, as soon as my trust fund matures or I hit the Megabucks jackpot.* I hear you. Would you feel better knowing that Steven Konkoly doesn't have a sandbag-reinforced compound on a lake in western Maine? Or a solar-powered battery system to feed Kate Fletcher's insatiable cappuccino habit in the face of a power outage? What if I told you that my basement stockpile doesn't resemble the "bunker" in Alex Fletcher's basement? This isn't a book about "keeping up with the Fletchers." Far from it. Preparedness doesn't have to involve $6,000 night vision scopes and an "all in or all out" mentality. I have neither—we'd rather take family vacations than watch deer creep through our yard at midnight, which is about the only use for night vision we'll likely encounter in our lives.

We've framed our attitude toward preparedness around balance and scale, two central concepts missing from the bulk of popular preparedness literature available today—*including my own fictional series based around Alex Fletcher!* Conversations with readers always lead to the same question. "Does your basement look like Alex Fletcher's?" Not even close, but if you braved the mess, you'd recognize many of the same elements found in Alex's bunker—on a much smaller scale.

This has often left me feeling a little guilty, especially since readers frequently tell me that they "learned something from my books" and "realize they are unprepared for a major disaster." Wow! Prepper-themed fiction is taken seriously by readers? Now I feel a responsibility to guide readers on a more reasonable disaster-planning journey. I accomplished my number one goal as a writer—to entertain. Time to take this journey a step further and fulfill the other half of the genre's bargain—to educate. Understanding the gravity of this undertaking, I decided to enlist some help.

Nobody embodies the right attitude about preparedness better than my co-author, Randy Powers. When I decided to write a book exploring the prepper and survival themes in *The Jakarta Pandemic* and *The Perseid Collapse* books, I couldn't think of a better partner. Randy's uniquely intelligent and nondogmatic approach to practical disaster preparedness and family independence won me over from the start. Randy explains how we met in his introduction, so I won't steal his thunder. He represents the epitome of how to prepare sensibly, and he does this professionally as a personal preparedness strategist at Practical Tactical. I'm thrilled to have him onboard for this project.

Another note about Randy. He knows more than I do about this topic. Not just a little more. A LOT MORE! I learn something new about preparedness, gardening or "life in general" every time I talk to him. Occasionally, he learns something from me—by accident, I imagine. That said, it is my sincere hope that you "walk away" from our book with the foundation to make impactful changes to your disaster preparedness situation. We'll point you in the right direction—if you want to take that first step. *We hope you do!*

Randall

Late in 2012, I discovered and devoured *The Jakarta Pandemic* by Steven Konkoly. Jakarta appealed to me acutely. I had long been aware of the threat a deadly pandemic would pose to the United States and had often wondered exactly how things would play out in my world as a result of a novel strain of a deadly virus bounding like wildfire across the country. The serene suburban life, almost completely dependent on the interconnectedness of our beautifully complex, just-in-time society to bring virtually everything we need right to our doorsteps, often with just the push of a button or a telephone call. What could possibly go wrong? If I am making a list of potential threats, a pandemic outbreak has always been right at the top. As I read the work, I thought to myself, "This guy gets it. I don't know if he believes everything he's talking about or not, but he gets it." So I decided to find out. I took a chance and sent Steve an email out of the blue with a request to do an interview for my blog. To my surprise, he not only responded to my email, but he was eager to talk about the work and excited about the interview process.

Over the course of our communications during the process of pulling together the interview for *Jakarta*, we each learned more about the other's thoughts on preparedness and most everything related to the end of the world as we know it. Along the way, Steve got a better feel for what we are all about at Practical Tactical, and I learned that he was considering bringing the Fletchers back in a new book. By the way, I quickly offered a few words of encouragement for the project! A while later, after he had sorted out the concepts for what would become *The Perseid Collapse* series of books, Steve asked if I would be interested in consulting on the books and lending a *prepper's eye* to the project. I readily agreed. When the opportunity came to work on a project I believed in with an author of Steve's talents, the decision to come on board was an easy one. We may make our homes at opposite ends of the Appalachian Trail, but when it comes to preparedness, we share a similar view.

A couple of months later, Steve pitched the idea of a collaborative effort based on the Fletchers that would be focused on their approach to preparedness. I am thrilled to be a part of such a wonderful opportunity to spread the word about preparedness and help others, regardless of where they are in their preparedness journey.

I believe in this project for several reasons. In the Fletchers' reality, Steve has crafted a fantastic framework that serves as a rich, real-world example of how anyone and everyone can go from a state of disorganization and unpreparedness to a condition of readiness and peace of mind that will allow you to navigate virtually any unexpected disaster situation by simply taking a few basic action steps. As we follow the Fletchers through their post-apocalyptic world, we can easily see the full spectrum of preparedness challenges that must be addressed. We are witness to how Alex and his crew address everything from the need for a basic home disaster kit, to how to travel and what you need to carry with you if you are forced to evacuate your home. Another thread that you see running throughout the preparedness plans of the Fletchers is the concept of resilience. Using what we consider to be the basic tenets of preparedness as a guide, Alex has built options into his preparedness plans, knowing that if it is important enough to have one of something when it comes to preparedness, it is better to have two. You know, just in case. Like that old saying goes, *"Two is one. One is none."*

How did I come to fully embrace the preparedness lifestyle? As a journalist, when I observe the world around me, I am driven to understand how and why things happen. The more I learned, especially regarding the "Three Es" (energy, the environment and the economy) and how those things work together, the more I felt compelled to get myself and the people I care about to a greater level of preparedness as quickly as possible. Pair this with an inherent tendency towards readiness carried over from my upbringing, and I guess you could say I was destined for it.

As I took the path less traveled in today's world of interconnected dependence, I learned and failed, and then learned and failed again. I pushed through to the other side and got myself to a good place regarding my personal level of preparedness using all of the skills (intellectual, physical and psychological) gathered over a lifetime, but countless times along my journey I wondered if anyone else out there found this concept of preparedness as overwhelming as I did, or if they felt the psychological impacts of truly understanding the necessity of this action as I had once the gravity of the situation became evident.

Through this process, the desire to learn gave way to action and then a need to share this information with others that may be beginning to head down the same path I started years ago. We simply wanted to help people because we believe in the practical need for preparedness as well as the positive impact it can have in our daily lives. This need manifested itself as Practical Tactical, our independently owned preparedness consulting business, where we take a holistic approach to personal preparedness and come at it from an absolutely apolitical position. We believe in taking a one-on-one approach to coaching the process of preparedness and crafting a plan to fit the needs of the individual, not the threat.

So, why write this book? Simply stated, it's what we're all about. We believe in the purpose and the process of preparedness and how those two things work together to shape our overall philosophy. Using the tools we lay out in this book, we know you can achieve your readiness goals. Thank you for choosing to allow us to be a part of your preparedness journey.

PART 2: FIRST STEPS

Chapter 1: ARE YOU A SURVIVOR?

Once the wave hit, they would assess and react accordingly. The decision to stay with the boat hadn't been an easy one. The safest course of action would have been to pack up as much gear and food as possible and ride the dinghy to the cove's southwestern shore. From there, a ten-minute walk would put them in one of the island's towering concrete World War Two lookout posts. While assuring their short-term safety, this option almost guaranteed they would lose their transportation off the island. He had considered putting Kate and the kids in the tower and taking his chances alone on the boat, but he had a feeling that the tsunami wasn't going to give him the option to return.

He planned to ride out the initial impact below deck, scrambling topside when the boat settled. He just hoped it wouldn't be too late to react at that point to save the boat. If the boat were dashed against the rocks before he could take control and engage the engine, they would be at the mercy of the elements, forced to swim back to the island.

—From *The Perseid Collapse*

Steven

Are you a survivor? Of course you are! We're all hardwired to survive. Faced with an immediate threat, like a swiftly moving forest fire while camping, nearly 100% of us will scoop up the little ones (beer cooler if you don't have kids) and run—or take some kind of emergency action with the hope of preserving our lives. Not every last minute decision will succeed, but most of us will give it our best try and hope for the best. If you continue to draw air after the harrowing experience, are you a survivor? Sure—sort of. One thing is certain. During your three-minute interview on national TV, you'll be hailed as a survivor. A LUCKY SURVIVOR. In most of the news segments I've watched, even the survivors admit they got lucky. They know it. You know it. Everyone knows it.

You never hear the story about the 99% of campers that stayed in the authorized camping zones, where rangers could easily find them and warn them about the sudden shift in winds that required immediate evacuation. Or the masses of campers who saw the fire danger warnings on the park service booking website and decided to change their weekend plans. Survivors just the same, just not as interesting. Unfortunately, we are bombarded day in and day out with the story of the LUCKY SURVIVOR—*and the impact of this media blitz is bad for your health.*

Mental role-play is a critical part of mental conditioning. When we watch a segment about the LUCKY SURVIVOR, we naturally role-play the final stages of the crisis, ignoring the earlier, avoidable stages. Who wants to stare into the middle distance over their coffee and bagel and imagine the sensible act of setting up your family tent in an authorized camping area, or canceling the reservation process when you see "highest fire danger hazard." Boring! I picture running to the nearest creek with my family, where we somehow leap into the water from a rock—holding hands as a wave of superheated air ignites the trees and bushes around us. I'm a hero! Right?

Here's the thing. If you asked a LUCKY SURVIVOR to choose between the two scenarios, they'd all go with the boring "don't book the trip" scenario, because on some level, we all understand that being the LUCKY SURVIVOR is not a sustainable strategy. It is especially not viable in terms of short- or long-term disaster preparedness. You might "luckily" survive the effects of the initial tsunami wave or the 8.9 Richter scale earthquake, *but luck has little place in the harsh reality that follows any natural disaster.*

The first step on the disaster preparedness journey is to recognize the difference between a LUCKY SURVIVOR and a DELIBERATE SURVIVOR. Once you understand the distinction, you can truly answer the question: ARE YOU A SURVIVOR? I hear a resounding YES! Does this mean you have to give up your daydreams about saving your family from the hoard of zombies surrounding your house? No. As long as you don't give up your family's seats on the last emergency airlift flight to the "safe zone" in order to retrieve your daughter's favorite stuffed animal. If your daydream includes the last part, we need to have a serious talk before you continue reading.

Randall

"Everything can be taken from a man but one thing: the last of the human freedoms–to choose one's attitude in any given set of circumstances, to choose one's own way." ~Viktor Frankl

Are you a survivor? What does that even mean, and how would you know?

A definition from Dictionary.com:

sur·vi·vor [ser-vahy-ver] noun **"a person who continues to function or prosper in spite of opposition, hardship, or setbacks."**

Not everyone is a survivor. This is the harsh truth, for any number of reasons. To be a survivor, you must first make the decision to survive. That decision is at the root of what we call the survivor mindset.

Without a doubt, the most critical factor in determining whether or not you are a survivor is whether you possess a survival mindset. Do you have the ability to identify a changing situation, honestly reassess your position, and then adjust your path forward based on new information? Do you have the resolve to do whatever it takes to ensure the safety and security of you and your family? Do you have the psychological resilience necessary to manage an ever-changing and uncertain future? If you don't know the answer to this question, you need to find out. Do not overlook the importance of cultivating a mindset that will allow you to face the challenges of survival.

I have a friend that recently wrestled with the concept of the survival mindset, and I was thrilled to see her work through the process of understanding and come to her own conclusions. Thankfully they were the correct ones! My friend, let's just call her LB, first became interested in preparedness after learning that I had started Practical Tactical, and she began asking questions about what we do. She had just become aware of a very popular television show based on the zombie apocalypse, and that was immediately where her mind went when we talked about anything relating to preparedness. When faced with such a complete and total collapse of society as her starting point when considering survival, she had decided there was no hope and that she would simply be *one of the first to die* in such a scenario. I immediately realized I needed to take a different approach in an attempt to walk her back from the edge a bit and change the lens through which she viewed preparedness. The more we talked, she quickly began to realize that there were countless real world and very practical reasons to prepare that had nothing at all to do with zombies and that she could absolutely do everything it took to *remain among the living*. Truly, all hope was not lost.

I am proud to report that since those first conversations where she was feeling totally overwhelmed and virtually hopeless, LB has made the decision to be a survivor and has made tremendous strides in her level of personal preparedness. After taking classes with Practical Tactical, she has put together a home disaster kit, a vehicle emergency kit and a basic BOLT kit, as well as taken training on the basics of firearms and self-defense. Although there is much more she wants to learn and accomplish, LB is a prime example of what it takes to be successful for anyone wanting to go from being scared to being prepared.

Chaos reigns during a time of disaster. Should you ever find yourself in a disaster situation, you will be thrust into a reality that is constantly evolving, and you have to be able to evolve with it. Resourcefulness is paramount, and the ability to improvise could prove to be a life-saving attribute in an emergency.

Survivors are often a mixture of opposites, balancing optimism with pessimism as two sides of the same coin. The ability to maintain a critical worldview yet retain self-confidence allows them to find the flaws in any plan, but still be able to see past them and seek a solution. Survivors are often rebels and not always comfortable following the rules. They tend to question authority and take an active role in affecting their own survival rather than waiting for instructions and do not spend a lot of time worrying about what has happened or what's been lost. Instead they choose to focus on the business of moving on, leaving behind the arresting emotions of loss, regret and disappointment.

The ability to improvise, to make due with what you have on hand, comes naturally to some, but it is also a skill that can be learned. You just have to train yourself to shake off the restrictive bonds of conventional thinking and look at things in a different way. When I was ten years old, I saw my dad do something that taught me this lesson in a way that I will never forget. My mom was working one evening, and my dad decided that he had a craving for cake. We had everything at home we needed to do some baking, and Dad decided to make it happen. Eventually, we came to the point that the cake batter needed to be blended, and Dad began to look for the handheld mixer. Dad didn't figure out until this point that he had no idea where the mixer was, a bit of poor planning on his part to be sure, and we were in a bit of a fix.

Since Mom was at work, we couldn't call her for a little help. There were no neighbors nearby, so we couldn't borrow a mixer, my brother and I were certainly no help, and all Dad could find were the detachable mixer blades. Sure, he could have mixed the batter by hand, but that wasn't how my dad had envisioned this process going, and now it was a challenge. We were in too deep to quit, and we didn't know how to move forward.

What's more, my dad, and now two kids aged ten and eight, wanted cake for dinner! That's when I saw my dad do something that changed my way of looking at problem solving forever. He had the detachable mixer blades, but we couldn't find the handheld mixer. What Dad could find was his power drill. Why not? Handheld mixer...power drill. Detachable mixer blades...drill bits. Seems like it should work, right? Sure enough, I watched my dad fit one of the detachable mixer blades into the end of his power drill and mix that cake batter like no cake batter had ever been mixed before. It took an experimental squeeze of the trigger or two to get the speed right, but Dad figured it out and got it done. A little while later, we were all eating chocolate cake and grinning ear to ear. For my dad, problem solved. For me, lesson learned. Since that day, I have known that I can do whatever needs to be done using only the resources available to me. The method may not be conventional, but that doesn't mean it can't be effective.

Too often, attitude and mental approach are formidable roadblocks for people interested in preparedness and developing a greater level of personal resilience. Another mental pitfall of preparedness is cognitive dissonance. Individuals take a look around, recognize that there are some pretty scary possibilities and trajectories out there, and they quickly become overwhelmed and simply shut down. When a threat seems too daunting, too large and damaging to our normal way of life, people often simply choose to ignore it. This is cognitive dissonance.

The co-conspirator to cognitive dissonance that proves to be the undoing of preparedness planning for a majority of the general populace is normalcy bias.

A definition and explanation from Wikipedia:

— The normalcy bias refers to a mental state people enter when facing a disaster. It causes people to underestimate both the possibility of a disaster occurring and its possible effects. This often results in situations where people fail to adequately prepare for a disaster, and on a larger scale, the failure of the government to include the populace in its disaster preparations. The assumption that is made in the case of the normalcy bias is that since a disaster never has occurred then it never will occur. It also results in the inability of people to cope with a disaster once it occurs. People with a normalcy bias have difficulties reacting to something they have not experienced before. People also tend to interpret warnings in the most optimistic way possible, seizing on any ambiguities to infer a less serious situation.

By reading this book, you are making a statement. You are a self-selected audience that has already prioritized the safety and security of you, your family and friends. We want to congratulate you for that! You've already crossed the biggest hurdle to preparedness, choosing to throw off the blinders of cognitive dissonance and reject the normalcy bias by recognizing that there are very real dangers in our world and that it is only prudent to take practical steps to mitigate the potential impacts from these threats on you and the ones you love.

However, simply acknowledging the realities of our world is not the end of the preparedness process, it is merely the beginning. Do you know you have the ability to follow through and take the actions necessary to actually survive a disaster situation? Can you simplify your life and prioritize, maintain perspective, and find a way forward through difficult times? Do you believe you can accomplish your goals, no matter the obstacles? The way to honestly answer these questions is to challenge yourself and put your often affirmative reflexive responses to the test.

An honest evaluation of your personal history could help as well. Maybe you know some things about yourself based on prior experience. Have you had occasions in your past where you've beaten the odds or faced down a daunting task and achieved it? If so, draw on that experience to remind yourself that you can be successful again.

Even if you have never been in that type of situation before, you can still learn something new about you. Knowledge is king. Once you have acknowledged the very real threats that are out there and educated yourself to the dangers associated with them, you are in a better position to assess your ability to deal with them. At this point, taking an open-minded approach and engaging in some mental gymnastics can offer some insight as well. Systematically running through scenarios in your mind and asking yourself a series of pointed "What if?" questions can often be a revealing process. Don't be afraid to push limits here. The further into the darkness you are willing to look, the more likely you are to learn something new about yourself.

As beneficial as they may be, mental calisthenics are no substitute for firsthand experience. Thinking about doing something and actually doing it are two very different things. To truly know what you are capable of, you must challenge yourself. This means challenging yourself physically and mentally. When faced with adversity, can you push through and overcome? Create scenarios and then put yourself through the paces to see how you deal with each situation. Whether we're talking about making tough calls regarding family and friends, the more physical aspects of survival like hiking five miles while wearing a forty-pound backpack, or even the most serious decisions like those regarding life and death, they all must be addressed. Thinking through these scenarios now, when making a mistake is not a matter of life and death, could prove to make all the difference should you ever have to make a similar decision in the future when it really counts.

To our way of thinking, the need to prepare is self-evident. Resourcefulness and the ability to adapt and improvise based on new information or circumstance, overcoming cognitive dissonance and the normalcy bias, as well as strengthening your situational awareness, resolve and psychological resilience is what the survival mindset is all about. Having faith in your abilities based on honest and earnest thought and practical experience will allow you to step forward into an uncertain future with confidence and optimism, knowing that you have answered difficult challenges in your past and that you can and will do so again.

Chapter 2: SURVIVE WHAT?

A sharp knock at the front door caused him to jump, spilling coffee on his hand.

"Damn it. Who the hell…?" he mumbled, setting the mug on the table.

He opened the door to find Charlie Thornton panting on his stoop. Charlie glanced over his shoulder twice, looking at the sky.

"They EMP'd our asses. Both of my cars are dead, and nothing works in my house. We're sitting ducks," said Charlie.

"Who EMP'd us?"

"The Chinese! Who else? They'll probably start landing paratroopers within the hour, like Red Dawn*!"*

Ed regarded his neighbor for a moment, hesitating to invite him inside. Charlie stood there barefoot, dressed in faded jeans and an oversized white Red Sox T-shirt. He clung nervously to a black, AR-style rifle fitted with some kind of scope. Ed wasn't keen on letting him inside, especially given the fact that Charlie had chosen a rifle over shoes.

"You gonna let me in or what? It won't be long before we're under direct attack," he said, looking past Ed. "My guess is we'll be hit by drones first."

—From *The Perseid Collapse*

Randall

In case you haven't noticed, there has been an explosion of post-apocalyptic dystopian fiction flooding the large and small screen in recent years. Zombies. Aliens. Asteroids. Any of it might make you think, "Being prepared? That sounds like a good idea." I would certainly agree, but the odds of any one of those things threatening you and your family any time soon are very long, to put it kindly.

This brings up the issue of event specific preparedness. Do you feel you need a target event to motivate you to get prepared? I can understand this way of thinking, to a point. Who hasn't watched an apocalyptic disaster movie and wondered to themselves, "What if that was me?" or, "What would we do in that situation?" A good movie or a well-written book can easily serve as the spark that gets you started on your journey to preparedness, and I'm all for it. Hey, whatever it takes to get you on the road to ready. But does that mean that you should limit your preparedness to focus on a singular event? I wouldn't recommend it. From our point of view, the bottom line goal is to strive to live a prepared lifestyle. This is what we're comfortable with, and it works for our family. The bright side to this approach is that if you're doing it right, you'll be more ready for anything that comes your way, and you will have achieved that new lot in life without turning your world upside down in the process. By simply accounting for each of the basic tenets of preparedness—shelter, water, food, fire, communications/defense and psychological readiness—in your everyday life with an eye towards setting yourself up to maintain and strengthen these in the future, we believe you will be ready to deal with and overcome whatever may come your way.

When you look around the preparedness landscape these days, there are several horses in the running to bring about the end of the world as we know it. Each a very real threat, each a very real possibility. However, when I think about preparedness, I'm thinking about the well-being of my family, right here and right now. We crowd-sourced a few of the most popular ideas, asking what may prove to be the trigger of our ultimate demise as a society, then took those ideas and distilled them down to a very personal level in an effort to show we need not look to a calamitous event on a national or worldwide scale for motivation to prepare.

The collapse of the US dollar, which could trigger a worldwide economic collapse, is something that we hear a lot about these days. That is certainly not a rosy scenario, but most people are far more worried about a personal economic collapse as the result of a job loss or a major injury that would prevent them from working. Taking steps to prepare now, like building an emergency food supply, can help lessen the impacts of an unexpected loss of income by helping stretch every dollar towards other needs should things get tight down the road, not to mention providing insurance against ever-rising food costs and inflation today.

Electromagnetic pulse (EMP), whether man-made or the result of a solar flare, is another terrible threat to our modern world. Should we be impacted by an EMP, we could see a human disaster on an almost unimaginable scale due to the loss of our electric grid. Without reliable electric power, our modern and extremely complex society would simply fail to operate. Considering the ramifications of this reality is truly terrifying. The harsh truth is we are so dependent on electric power coming to us at the flip of a switch that an event resulting in an extended power outage can become a localized disaster very quickly. Unfortunately we see this type of situation all across the United States every year as a result of severe weather or infrastructure failure. If you did not have power in your home for a week or more, how would you be impacted? Would you have the ability to heat your home, prepare your meals or keep up with the latest news about the situation in your area? By developing a plan today and building resilience into your life before disaster strikes, you will be able to mitigate the impacts of an emergency situation that might turn into a full-blown disaster for someone that was not prepared.

Terrorism is a scourge that we live with every day in the United States since the attacks of September 11, 2001. The possibility that there could be another attack, possibly a dirty bomb or some other NBC (nuclear, biological, chemical) attack, looms over us all and is just a fact of life in twenty-first century America. Whether it originates from somewhere overseas or is homegrown, there is not much the average citizen can do to stop this threat. However, there is another threat that is just as dangerous, has a long and terrible history in this country, and is just as likely that cannot be overlooked, and that is civil unrest or riots. America has witnessed violent protests time and again over the years, and they often prove to be just as senseless as any act of terrorism, except this threat could actually begin right in our neighborhood. Given the right circumstances, mobs of people acting without restraint and with no fear of any reprisal could swarm your area and create an extremely dangerous situation for you and your family in a very short amount of time. Do you have an evacuation or escape plan if your neighborhood or home were in the suddenly defined danger zone? Would you be able to defend yourself or your loved ones if the wolves were at your door? Threats like this that come right out of the blue are the types of events that we believe make the need to be prepared self-evident, and you do not have to look hard to see them.

What about disaster on a timeline? What if you knew when a major disaster was going to strike? Would it make a difference in how you chose to prepare? For us, it doesn't really matter. We adopted a preparedness lifestyle years ago and do our best to improve our level of readiness every day. Suddenly finding out that there was a super volcanic eruption scheduled for 3:45 pm next Thursday wouldn't change anything for us. It would, however, trigger a vigorous assessment of our current plans as we processed the new information. From there, we would adapt accordingly and do the best we could as we moved forward.

But, that's us. We're already working towards a level of preparedness that we have determined is appropriate for our family and our situation. On the other hand, what if you're not already well on your way to being ready for zombie aliens, or any other life-altering event, for that matter? What if you've done virtually nothing to be ready to deal with an emergency situation, whether it is on a global, national, regional or local scale? What if you haven't taken the steps necessary to insulate yourself against even an unexpected upheaval in your personal life like the loss of a job or a serious injury to you or a family member? What if there was an extended power outage or civil unrest in your area? What if you knew ahead of time that this tumult was coming? Would that knowledge motivate you to change your behavior? Of course it would. The question is, why not save yourself some stress and headache and go ahead and take some basic steps to mitigate the impacts of any emergency that may come to you down the road?

Why should it matter if you know when the "big bad" is going to show up? If you would fight the crowds to get the supplies you and your family would need in the chaos of the moment that will surely accompany any such event, why not prepare now to remove yourself from the panic equation later? By getting your ducks in a row today, you will be free to assess the situation, then adapt and implement your plans that were made without the proverbial gun to your head, with a clear purpose in the moment, and greatly increase your ability to make it through to the other side of any future emergency event.

So why not get started today? We love zombies. We love aliens. Space weather, we love that too. Whatever feeds your fire and motivates you to get prepared, we're all for it, but realize that you don't have to look very hard to find plenty of reasons to get prepared. Just get started. You'll be well on your way to ready before you know it, and I'm betting you'll be surprised at how satisfying your journey will be along the way.

Steven

I mentioned the upcoming zombie apocalypse at the end of the first chapter for a reason. **It's coming!** Why else would someone buy 20,000 rounds of .223 ammunition? Zombies don't kill themselves, at least not on AMC's *The Walking Dead* series. Seriously, I've seen discussions about large ammunition purchases, in the 20,000 range and higher, on prepper and survival forums. I have no idea what kind of bulk deal you get when you buy that much ammunition online, but at the going rate, the purchase described above would set you back about $7,000! And you still have to buy four years of dehydrated food for four people at $7,000 a year. Personally, I think we can cut down on the ammunition, but that's my often unpopular opinion. *Here's where it gets fun.*

Who wants to have a spirited, made-up discussion about post-apocalyptic survival? I know I have a few takers, not that any of you really have a choice. Here we go.

Some of you might be saying—*Steve, ammunition will be scarce in the lawless world soon to envelop us. Better to get it now.*

I retort—*U.S. Marines fighting an extended close-quarters battle during the second battle of Fallujah often didn't expend their initial load-out of 210–300 rounds (7–10 magazines)…and they fought for days on end.*

Your excellent response to my imaginary dialogue—*You can also use ammunition to trade for food and essential supplies.*

Me—*Fair point! That cuts down on the amount I'll need to spend on dehydrated food and MREs, though I'd be cautious about giving ammunition to anyone in lawless times.*

You—*I never thought about that aspect of the situation. I guess we should only buy 15,000 rounds.*

Me—*Well, since you're not going to buy all 20,000, maybe I should buy the other 5,000.*

Is anyone thinking…THESE TWO ARE CRAZY! WHAT ARE THEY EVEN TALKING ABOUT? If this thought crossed your mind at any point in my pretend conversation, you've sort of passed the test. At the very least, you realized that it's preposterous to prepare for the zombie apocalypse—and not just because zombies aren't real. Hopefully, you thought, "Man, this seems like overkill," or, "No way I'm spending that much on prepping."

Despite these reasonable thoughts, I'm willing to bet at some point during the conversation you felt the "fever," if just fleetingly for a moment. Everyone gets the "fever" or the prepping "bug," because it's hard to put a price on readiness or survival. Right? And that price has no limit in today's society, beyond the remaining equity in your house and your credit rating, ***especially if you let the "fever" dictate the SCALE and BALANCE of your preparedness goals.***

You can control the "fever" by asking yourself: **SURVIVE WHAT?** If your answer to this question is "a lethal pandemic, which triggers an opportunistic EMP attack by China, followed immediately by a government-assisted United Nations takeover," then I have bad news for you. Planning for the "Big Kahuna" scenario will require trust-fund-level resources or a lucky break at the casino boats. Most of you should have answered: blizzard, flooding, tornado, earthquake, wildfire, hurricane or an extended power outage probably caused by one of the preceding answers. That's the short list, because every year we can count on Mother Nature to deliver.

How did the author of *The Jakarta Pandemic* originally answer SURVIVE WHAT? In southern coastal Maine, the most common threat to our comfort zone is a "Nor'easter." You have to use a strong Maine accent to say it right. We're talking about a nasty, protracted storm marked by high winds and heavy precipitation. They typically arrive in the late fall thru early spring, when the temperatures are below or barely above freezing. Nor'easters frequently kill the power and create unsafe travel conditions for an extended period of time. My most immediate survival/readiness need is the ability to safely stay in my home for seven to ten days in the middle of January, when temperatures could drop below zero degrees Fahrenheit. This is where the author of *The Jakarta Pandemic* started. I took slow, measurable steps to achieve this goal.

Once I had covered the basics for my most likely disaster scenario—*I treated the family to 20,000 rounds of ammunition!* Just kidding. I patted myself on the back and took a look at expanding my readiness to handle a scenario less likely to occur, but more difficult to endure (more on that scenario later). Interestingly, the "preps" required to meet this new challenge didn't follow a simple, linear progression. Cost and effort skyrocketed.

I'm glad I didn't start with the less likely scenario. Why? Get ready for a cliché. *When we bite off more than we can chew, we tend to spit out the whole mess.* That's fine if you've decided to rebuild the weed-infested, vintage 1967 Mustang your dad left sitting in the barn for thirty years, only to realize two weeks into the project that it's going to cost you $15,000 and 2,000 hours of time that you don't have. No loss. **Disaster preparedness is too important to spit out because you took a monster bite.**

Trust me, the SCALE and BALANCE of disaster preparedness can spiral out of control from the start if you get caught up in the "fever" and tackle more than you can handle financially or time-wise. At the end of the day, you'll have tricked-out, matching his and hers AR-15s; 20,000 rounds of questionable ammunition; generation III night vision goggles, because the cheap Russian knockoff stuff is for amateurs; and four years of dehydrated food packed in 144 plastic buckets—all stored in a basement that completely floods twice a year because your $400 sump pump "ain't cutting it."

SURVIVE WHAT? Answer this question realistically, and you've taken one of the biggest steps in the right direction.

Chapter 3: GETTING STARTED

"You're going too fast for the kids. A regular walking pace would work better, especially with the heat. These packs will feel twice as heavy by the time we reach Highland Avenue."

Kate sensed that he didn't want to fight, so she accepted his suggestion and slowed the pace. He could have argued the physics of how the tsunami might have reached their house with more force, or continued on the all-or-nothing survivor mentality track, but he had opted for more constructive counsel. After more than twenty years of marriage, subtle shifts in tone and commentary often carried more meaning and significance than an obvious, outward expression. In this case, she interpreted it as a temporary concession. She'd take it. They needed to work together from this point forward.

"Yep. I can feel this damn thing digging into my shoulder already. They're not exactly the most comfortable packs. How long do you think it will take us to get home?" she asked, slowing down to fall into step beside him.

"Five miles? I'd say two to three hours, depending on the burden of these packs and the temperature. That's assuming we can follow the usual roads, which is a fair assumption. Even if the water made it that far inland, we shouldn't be looking at anything more than an occasional downed tree or power line—maybe some debris. We should be home before the day gets ridiculously hot."

"Sounds like fun. This isn't exactly the weight-loss plan I had in mind, but I'll take what I can get," Kate said, adjusting the pack on her shoulders.

—From *The Perseid Collapse*

Steven

Is your finger hovering over the "Buy" button on the 365-day supply of dehydrated food yet? I hope not. We need to spend a little more time talking about the philosophy of preparedness before Randy and I turn you loose on the complacent, unprepared world surrounding us. Remember the question posed in Chapter 2? SURVIVE WHAT? Let's start there and make a candid assessment of where you stand—today.

You might be surprised by how basic this assessment needs to be, and how easy it is to make a false assumption early in the planning process. Here's a great illustration of what I mean. I've watched one episode of *Doomsday Preppers*, which featured a middle-aged guy planning to "bug out" of his neighborhood on foot. He had a Bug Out Bag or BOLT kit (more on BOLT later), weather-appropriate clothing, good footwear and a self-defense item. What could go wrong? How about a heart attack! At the beginning of the show, he could barely walk down the block without having to sit down and take several breaks!

And this was without his backpack. I think the guy on the show was single, but his dilemma sparked a ton of thought. What about his wife? Can she lug a backpack twenty miles? Can the kids even walk five miles without a backpack on a muggy summer day? Mine can't—unless we're headed toward an ice cream shop. This is the challenge we all face creating a disaster preparedness plan. The simplest tasks require extreme honesty about the most basic skills and assumptions. This is why I strongly recommend you start out small and expand your plan once you've covered the fundamentals.

I'll make a confession here. When I saw that guy huffing and puffing around his block, I felt a little smug. I'm in pretty good shape (in my own mind) for a forty-three-year-old. I can walk up and down stairs without getting winded, and I can certainly walk five to ten miles without collapsing—but could I do it with thirty to fifty pounds of gear in the middle of the summer? Sure...I think. I could do it fifteen years ago at Camp Pendleton with the U.S. Marine Corps. Fifteen years ago! Yikes, who's not being honest now?

How many of us overestimate our abilities or our readiness? I bet the percentage is high. Unfortunately, the heat index doesn't care if you slightly overestimated your endurance—neither does the weight on your back. Their judgment is objective and merciless. You need to take the same approach and make a candid assessment of where you stand financially, physically, mentally and equipment-wise compared to your SURVIVE WHAT scenario.

Did I mention Buy In? I know Randy will. I'm actually so confident that he'll cover it in detail I'll keep my two cents short and sweet. Everyone immediately affected by your disaster readiness plan needs to fall somewhere above "this is stupid" on the Buy-In scale. They don't have to eagerly volunteer to carry an extra eight pounds (1 gallon) of water on your planned exodus from town, but they need to be in a mental place where they won't purposely unravel the plan. *If you can't rely on everyone directly involved in the plan, then you need to revise the plan*—or invest in a wheelbarrow and duct tape. That was a joke. I don't recommend duct-taping your wife (or kids) to a wheelbarrow and pushing them to your destination. Too much effort, and it might attract the attention of local authorities.

Randall

Once you have looked around our everyday world and decided to take steps to become more prepared, the next step is to assess your situation...honestly. You may think you have already considered everything you have to account for, but a second look will most likely reveal some things you missed. Overconfidence in the abilities of yourself or others in your group is one of the most common mistakes people make when thinking about preparedness. Can you really hike five miles with that fifty-pound pack on your back? Will your kids hike that far wearing their packs? Have you tried it to make sure? Do you even know what gear you need? Maybe your plan is to load up the family along with everybody's gear and drive the sixty miles out of the city to Aunt Jill's house in a disaster situation. Sounds good. Will all of your gear fit into the vehicle? Does everyone even know what they need to take? If your primary evacuation route is impassable due to traffic congestion or damage from the event, do you have another plan? Oh, wait! What about the dog? This situation could get really ugly, really fast.

Of course, all of this is assuming everyone in your family or group is on the same page about preparing. Maybe your wife or husband doesn't see the need in even having a disaster plan because they are an optimist or they don't want to waste their time worrying about things that are out of their control. What if your children cannot be bothered to learn the family disaster plan? Maybe they just don't believe anything bad will ever happen and if something does happen, someone will be there to help. The Red Cross or the Salvation Army. FEMA. The government. I mean, isn't that why we pay taxes?

Building a dependable team and getting everyone on board with your preparedness planning is the key to success. This task may seem daunting, but if the safety of your family or group is important enough to take steps to prepare, the time and hard work it will take to get everyone to buy in to the plan is worth it, and your team will be that much stronger for it in the end. There is no one way to go about accomplishing this goal because every situation, every person, is different. The secret to your success in getting everyone to commit to the process is to remember that there is a key that will unlock each individual's participation. It's just up to you to find it. Remember, you know these people, and you want them with you for a reason. You already know how to reach out to them, how to appeal to them. Everyone processes things differently, so think it through and use every tool at your disposal to get the job done, whatever it may be. Some folks respond to logic; others are led by their heart. Maybe there is a part of preparedness that an unfocused team member is really interested in. Use that to your advantage. Plausible fiction is a fantastic way to open people's minds to the need to prepare. A realistic movie based on a natural disaster or deadly flu virus or a good book with a preparedness theme may be exactly the way to bring someone around to your way of thinking. What you should absolutely not do is beat someone over the head with the idea of prepping for an emergency. Telling someone that if they don't listen to you and do exactly what you say they are going to die is no way to win people over. Instead, rely on talking to your friend or family member in a way that will appeal to them on a personal level. Everyone wants to reach their own conclusions, especially when it comes to something as important and involved as preparedness, so trust that you can reach them and give them the space to do just that. Above all else, always be honest with them. This topic and the safety of everyone involved demands nothing less. At the end of the day, you may not be able to reach everyone and bring them on board. In some cases, it may simply be better to wish one another good luck and part ways. This should not be the goal, but it may be a reality. By being honest with yourself and any potential members of your group, you give everyone involved the best chance for a successful partnership. But if that is just not possible, at least everyone can make the decision that is best for them based on reliable information. That is all anyone can reasonably ask in any situation.

Chapter 4: PLANNING

"We have a lot of prep work to do. Bicycles, backpacks, and weapons are first priority. The rescue group needs two packs. One BOLT bag and a smaller assault kit—"

"What's an assault kit?" asked Ed. "I don't have stuff like that."

"It's just a smaller backpack, like this," said Alex, lifting up the dark green, nylon backpack from the side of his chair.

"We'll use these when we leave the car to get the kids. Nothing but the basics. Ammo, water, limited food, first aid kit...it's all here on the sheets."

"Why pack two bags?" asked Linda.

"The BOLT bags are for situations requiring us to permanently abandon the Jeep. We'll be able to continue on foot with enough supplies to get us to our destination," Alex explained.

"What if that happens before you reach Boston?"

"The mission remains the same. Get the kids and get back to Limerick. The only parameter that changes is the length of time it takes to accomplish the mission. Could be twelve hours, could be twelve days."

"Are you sure you're up for this, Charlie?" Linda asked her husband.

"Of course I'm up for this! What the hell are you talking about?"

"If the car dies in Sanford, Maine, you're looking at what," she made a quick calculation using the map, "a hundred and fifty mile round trip on foot?"

"Then I'll finally lose that last ten pounds!"

"What about your knee—and your back?"

"I'll bring my knee wrap and back brace, along with plenty of pain meds. I hike through the woods for days on end up in the county looking for deer. I'll be fine. It's these two beach strollers I'm worried about—gotcha there, guys," said Charlie.

—From *The Perseid Collapse*

Randall

When it comes to personal preparedness, there is much to consider. Everything from figuring out what you're preparing for and why, to what you're going to do and what you need to get it done. It can be overwhelming. With all of the variables involved with disaster preparedness, it is very easy to get sidetracked from your original goal, and that can lead to frustration, thereby slowing your progress. To our way of thinking, the key to unlocking a successful preparedness strategy is to keep things rational, informed and in order. You need to bring organization to a process associated with chaos. In other words, you need a plan!

Before you spend one penny on gear, start forming a survival group, or break ground on that new backyard bunker, you should start at the beginning and focus on you...your situation, your options and your needs. This is not a deal where keeping up with the Joneses will do you any good. In fact, it might get you killed. The color of their grass does not matter. Your disaster preparedness plan should be personalized, tailored to fit what's going on in your world right now. How many people are in your family or group? Are there any special diet, health or age considerations? Does anyone bring a specialized skill set to your group? Any consideration to what your situation will be six months from now is not your immediate concern and should not be your focus. You cannot afford to develop a plan based on where you hope you will be six months from now or what you would like to have. A miscalculation like this could prove fatal. You must be honest with yourself and construct your plan based on the facts as you know them today. You can always adjust any plan as new information or assets become available. Part of that consideration is identifying the hazards that currently pose the biggest threat to you and your area. This information will help you scale your response to the appropriate level. As you think through your planning, you will begin to identify the best options for you and your family or group. Answers to such questions as "What situations would force us to leave our home or our city?" or "Where will we go if we're forced to evacuate, and how will we get there?" will begin to come into focus. Once you've identified the questions that need to be answered, you can start to work out the answers as well as what exactly it will take to make those answers a reality.

We have a phrase for this bottom-up, pyramid approach to the planning process. At Practical Tactical, we like to "Kit to Fit." This refers to part of the Practical Tactical Cycle, which we will discuss in more detail later. In short, it is a process of education and assessment, developing a personalized preparedness plan and then building your kit to fit your plan as opposed to working things the other way around, followed up with training and evaluation. Many times, people get so caught up in all of the flashy and "tacti-cool" gear associated with preparedness that they lose focus.

A common mistake someone new to preparedness will make is to go out and buy a bunch of expensive gear because they saw it on some website or television show, conveniently overlooking the fact that in most cases they don't know how to use said gear, stack it in a big pile when they get home, and proceed to haphazardly make a plan to suit the gear they have on hand. Of course, that's assuming they understand the need to give any thought to planning at all.

This is a recipe for disaster based on the comforting marketing promise that if you have all the neat stuff, somehow that will make you invincible to the realities of survival. We disagree. We believe that developing a personalized plan based on your situation before you give any thought to outfitting yourself and your family or group will save you time, money and more than one headache down the road. In the end, you will be left with a more flexible and functional plan. A plan that you have an intimate knowledge of and a comfortable confidence in that will make your odds of success exponentially better. Plus, you will most likely still have plenty of really cool gear at your disposal. That's just one of the perks of preparedness. Regardless of whether you are focused on the overall disaster plan or just one part of your plan, like getting back home if you are away when a disaster strikes, the same process will always apply.

As an example, let's take a look at a situation we had to deal with in developing our family disaster plan. After we did the research, developed a disaster plan for our home, complete with evacuation plans, and got ourselves squared away with the gear necessary to execute our plan, my wife and I started thinking about what we would do if we were away from home when a disaster strikes. You can have the best plan in the world and all the preps to execute it perfectly at your home, but if you cannot get back to your "insurance policy," it will be worth about as much as a whistle in the wind. We knew we had a new challenge to tackle.

We both work away from home and commute to work every day. Not only do we travel in polar opposite directions to go to work, I have to travel more than twice the distance one way than my wife does just to get there. It was clear. Should we find ourselves in an emergency situation while on the job, we would each be on our own to get home. Once we knew the score, we applied the concepts of the Practical Tactical Cycle and proceeded to build our kits to get home to fit each of our individual plans.

This is just one example of a circumstance that requires a little extra planning. Just looking within my family, I can see other examples that are just as demanding as ours, if not more. My mom has physical limitations, and my brother has two very young children to consider when developing his preparedness plan. These are very real challenges, but they can be overcome. The key is to educate yourself about the factors impacting your situation, recognize the challenges in your preparedness plan early on, and address them head on before they cost you something infinitely more valuable than a few dollars, like your life or the life of a friend or loved one.

Steven

Now that you've come clean and admitted that you need a few more laps around the track (I'll be right behind you)—it's time to buy all the gear you'll need to survive the apocalypse! Finger off the "buy" button! Sorry to do that to you again. I promise there will come a point in this book where you can mouse-click a button that will send your spouse or significant other through their first Buy-In crisis. Patience. We have a few more First Steps to take in the planning process—like come up with a plan.

I joke about buying gear in each chapter for a reason—to prepare you for a mind-blowing piece of wisdom. When you hear the words "mind-blowing" in one of these essays, it usually means Randy introduced me to it. Are you sitting down? Here it comes. ***Develop your plan before deciding what gear you need***. I hear crickets—probably because this messes up your plan to get a National Firearms Act (NFA) tax stamp to buy that fully automatic AR-15 you've been eyeballing on Gunbroker.com. I know it stings. Stings for me too. While Randy didn't invent the concept of planning from the ground up, he did bring the phrase "Kit to Fit" to the readiness game. It's catchy, and it embodies nearly everything I have to say about the planning process. You build a Kit to Fit your plan.

But that's not fun, Steven! What if my plan only requires me to add twenty cans of food and a basic first aid kit to my basement storage shelves? How does that get me any closer to the AR-15 with EOTech holographic sight that I NEED? It doesn't, but if a few cans of food and a first aid kit are truly all you need to endure the most likely disaster scenario threatening your family, you can buy the rifle—after you shell out $50 at the grocery store. See, I told you we'd be friends again!

This may seem like a rudimentary, almost silly example of Kit to Fit, but I guarantee your town is filled with folks sporting full gun safes and empty pantry shelves. They didn't fail the Kit to Fit test. They never showed up to take the test. Most of these people haven't seriously considered a disaster preparedness plan, which would better balance the contents of the safe and pantry. Frankly, this group scares me the most. Twenty days into a crisis that cripples our nation's food-delivery system, these folks are going to reverse Randy's catch phrase. Fit the Kit will define their new survival strategy. When your Kit consists solely of an AR-15, hunting is your only option. Let's hope they go hunting outside of your neighborhood.

Once again, I hit you with a slightly overdramatized example of the concept. Roving bands of hungry, firearms-toting citizens—with no plan. I just scared myself into buying another case of ammunition and made a good case for purchasing a firearm as part of your disaster readiness plan. We'll talk about that in more detail later.

Let's talk about the less obvious problem with putting the "cart before the horse" and buying up all of that fancy survival gear before you figure out what you truly need to execute your personal readiness plan. ASSUMPTION. Fill your basement with survival and preparedness gear right now, before you develop a plan, and I guarantee you will make one of two dangerous assumptions about readiness.

The most common assumption will be an excited and proud "I'm ready!" Ready for what? The assumption crumbles as you stutter through a list of scenarios, none of which match up to your SURVIVE WHAT disaster. This is easy to remedy. You pretend the pile of gear doesn't exist and create a plan, ultimately comparing what you need to what you have. Make the adjustments and you're back on the Kit to Fit path.

The less common, more insidious assumption will be a subconscious version of Fit the Kit, where the "prepper" thinks they've followed the process, but have let the Kit cloud their judgment. This comes in a few forms:

Overconfidence in your abilities based on the quality and quantity of equipment. An expensive rifle and night vision goggles don't make you a candidate for Delta Force. In most cases, they turn you into one more guy stepping on branches at night while trying to move your family through sketchy territory.

Developing the wrong plan based on what you have. It worked for MacGyver! And the dozen or so writers scribbling furiously to ensure MacGyver's plan succeeded. Given a set of equipment, human nature ensures that your plan will reflect the contents of your readiness "bunker" and not the other way around. You aren't MacGyver, and you don't have Steven Konkoly making sure that your character survives.

I feel like I've beaten this one to death. You get the picture. "Kit to Fit." "Plan from the ground up." "Plan first, gear later." "Hear me now, listen to me later." What? Just checking to make sure your eyes haven't completely glazed over. However you want to say it, just DO IT.

PART 3: THE BASICS

Chapter 5: FRAMEWORK

Kate let go of the mop and grabbed her rifle from one of the coat hooks in the mudroom. She slung it over her shoulder and let it hang in the "shoulder-ready" position behind her back, where it was out of the way, but readily accessible. The rifle no longer felt like a cold, alien object. It still caught on furniture and clunked against the walls, but she'd come to terms with the fact that the rifle wasn't dangerous, unless she released the safety and pulled the trigger.

The kitchen looked spotless, if you could overlook a few structural problems. Split cabinets, cracked backsplash tile, missing chunks of drywall, painted over bloodstains, and bullet peppered furniture to name a few. Still, it was a radical improvement over this morning. She could live with the cosmetic damage, especially if it meant they could stay. The realities of evacuating the house weighed heavily on her mind.

They had designed the compound with resilience and redundancy in mind. "The rule of three's." Three sources or layers for each of their basic needs. Water provided by a well, pumped out of the pond or collected in 50 gallon, food grade drums from the gutters during a rainstorm. Food supplied by their garden and fields, supplemented when necessary by the vast stores in the basement, with the year round option of fishing, trapping or hunting. Security had multiple layers. Communications. Heating. Power. Whenever practical, they sought long-term solutions with multiple back ups. If they left Gelder Pond, their survival plan would have to fit into a car—shared by another family.

—From *Event Horizon*

Steven

I feel like I've spent most of my time writing these essays in a confessional booth. I've finally committed a cardinal collaborative writing sin—I took an advanced peek at Randy's essay for this chapter. Eloquently written, succinctly stated, thoroughly explored—and I see he used graphics. Graphics? Come on, I don't have any graphics! What? This isn't a contest? Somebody tell Randy this, because he beat me hands down—as I expected.

Framing the survival basics is the bread and butter of Randy's business, which is why he succeeds and excels as a personal readiness coach. This framework serves as your "readiness lens" to view and navigate the more detailed chapters. Sort of a springboard into the deep end, where you get to explore the different aspects of disaster preparedness without arm floaties. You can still have those if you want! We keep a ready supply by the side of the pool.

The importance of a solid framework can't be understated. No matter which topic you explore, your approach should be the same. Start with the minimum level of readiness preps you need to endure your SURVIVE WHAT scenario and expand from there, as long as that expansion doesn't cannibalize another critical area. We cover a lot of ground in the next eleven foundational chapters. Your initial SURVIVE WHAT scenario might not require you to take action in all eleven categories. Mine didn't. Not even close. But my next scenario required a significant amount of work in ALL categories. I guarantee the next scenario on your disaster preparedness continuum will too.

Building a strong foundation in each of the eleven categories paves the way toward flexibility in your readiness planning. Resilience through redundancy follows. Sounds like the underpinnings of a PhD level "prepper" philosophy course, right? Let me break it down into something Alex Fletcher and Steven

Konkoly have understood long before either of them heard the word "prepper." RULE OF THREES.

The RULE OF THREES boils down to purposeful and useful REDUNDANCY. You see it everywhere in the military, which is why I immediately recognized its usefulness as a readiness tool. Military redundancy serves a distinct purpose. It keeps troops in the fight and saves lives. *Sounds like a system tailor-made for disaster preparedness.* Let's take a quick look at a military example. Hold on while I put on my technothriller hat. I love writing about this stuff.

At my first duty station, a frigate homeported in Japan, redundancy spanned the vessel from fore to aft, down to the very structural design of the ship. All of the critical control stations were separated by enough distance to prevent the command and control functions of the ship from being wiped out by a single detonation. The ship's throttle and steering could be transferred from the bridge to engineering. Steering could be done from the rudder itself. Damage control (fighting hull breaches and fires) could be conducted from one of several stations. Yeah, yeah, closing watertight hatches, sticking wooden plugs in holes and spraying water at fires. What about the weapons, you ask? The epitome of focused redundancy.

The weapons systems formed a layered defense against antiship missiles and other threats. Long-range surface-to-air missiles reached out to forty miles, followed by a 76mm rapid-fire, radar-controlled cannon that took over the fight at five miles, capped by the 20mm Phalanx Close-in-Weapons (CIWS) capable of firing 4,500 rounds per minute at anything that survived the other two systems. I was the fourth layer of defense, firing an M-14 from the bridge wing. That's not true, but I would have volunteered to do this. Sadly, they rarely let me carry a weapon during my tour of duty—they knew better.

A U.S. warship is a far cry from your home, but the concept of redundancy still applies. Three alternatives. A primary, secondary and emergency means of satisfying each requirement of your plan. Randy takes it a step further and talks about scale within the RULE OF THREES. *Redundancy to scale.* PhD-level stuff for sure, but easy to understand with my help. Another military example coming right up.

If you take a close look at a U.S. Marine Corps infantryman's kit, you'll see the RULE OF THREES, and I'm not talking about the requirement for more than three tattoos. *Marines like tattoos— fact.* I told you we'd learn something. I spent four years working alongside marines, so I get to make a few jokes at their expense. Beyond the three-tattoo minimum, all of their essential gear is based on redundancy. Nothing demonstrates Randy's redundancy to scale concept than the load-bearing equipment issued to a marine.

The Family of Improved Load Bearing Equipment (FILBE) consists of three layers:

1. A large, framed Main pack, which holds all of a marine's field equipment. When a marine goes into the field, they stuff their life into this pack. This usually sits in their tactical vehicle or Forward Operating Base.

2. A smaller, internal frame Assault pack, which is designed to be worn on extended missions. We typically refer to the Assault pack as a 72-hour pack. Marines stuff it with MREs, water, extra ammunition, anything they'll need to stay alive in a hostile environment. They will typically drop this at a designated point prior to attacking the enemy.

3. The final layer is the tactical rig, which consists of the body armor vest, belt, holster, anything strapped directly to the marine's body. Attached to the tactical rig, you'll find most of their ammunition, a water hydration bladder (CamelBak), grenades, Motorola and personal first aid kit. Everything marines need in a firefight. When assaulting an enemy position or patrolling a hostile valley, the tactical rig might be all they carry.

FILBE is a multilayered system designed to accomplish the same mission (carry a marine's gear) in a variety of environments. It's no mistake that I use a lot of military-designed equipment in my personal readiness load-out.

There, I added something to the discussion. Not easy to do with Randy on the job.

Randall

Once you have taken an honest measure of where you are, the threats you should be preparing for, and you have weaved your family disaster plan around this framework, it is time to make sure you have what you need to execute your plan. We have established some useful tools to help you sort through the myriad of options you will have to choose from at every level of preparedness.

As we mentioned in the last chapter, you should start at the beginning and focus on you…your situation, your options and your needs. Well, starting at the beginning means starting with the basics. Whether we are talking about your family disaster plan or larger questions like whether you can or should stay at your home during a disaster situation, we have a system that will help bring clarity to your decision-making process.

In disaster preparedness there are certain factors that must be dealt with if you want to affect a positive result for you and your family or group. At Practical Tactical, we know these as the basic tenets of preparedness: shelter, water, food, fire, communications, defense and psychology. If you are going to mitigate the impacts on your team during any disaster situation, each of these basic concepts must be identified and addressed. This is your starting point for determining your preparedness needs from a "big picture" perspective. Taking the time to identify the basic concepts will steer your choices as you narrow your field of focus down to a personal level for you and each member of your family or group later.

Our philosophy on personal preparedness is one of layers, with each layer building another level of resilience into your overall preparedness plan. As you work your way through the process, you will see how all of the pieces (or layers) work together to reinforce your efforts in pursuit of the ultimate goal, which is to keep you and your loved ones safe and mitigate the impacts of any disaster.

Every personal preparedness plan begins with a family disaster plan that will cover what you and every member of your household will do in case of an emergency at your home or a disaster situation in which you will be able to shelter in place. Because disaster does not care about the clock or what is convenient for your schedule, you must be prepared to respond at all times and in all situations. As an acknowledgement to this reality, it is prudent to have a plan of attack should events conspire to force you out of your home. This will require an entirely different set of plans and a corresponding set of adjustments to your kit. If disaster were to strike while you are not at home, you would be forced to transition quickly to a plan that will move you away from the threat and simply make it back to your home to link up with your family or group. This is yet another scenario that requires a different set of plans and gear.

Is your head spinning yet? Well, don't worry. Everything is about to fall into place. This may all sound like a lot of planning and gear, and you may even wonder if all of that is really necessary. The answer is yes. Regardless of whether you're building a home disaster kit or a set of mobile gear designed to help you survive a situation that forces you to be on the move, they are all based on the basic tenets of preparedness we laid out earlier. We believe in living by the "Rule of Three," which states you should have at least three ways to accomplish any goal, and that filters into our thoughts on preparedness as well. Because of this fact, there will be some overlap built into the kits, but how you choose to cover each tenet should be scaled to fit the purpose of that particular kit. For example, you may have a generator, a large flashlight and the ability to make fire in your home disaster kit, but you may carry a pocket-sized light, a headlamp and an emergency glow stick in your mobile kit to lessen the weight or to keep your hands free while on the move. Both setups will provide you with options for a light source should you need one, but the items chosen for each particular kit are based on what provides you the greatest tactical advantage in that situation. By approaching preparedness in this manner, not only are you covering your immediate survival needs, but you are also systematically building redundancy into your gear and resilience into your overall preparedness planning.

Tackling a concept as large and as multifaceted as disaster preparedness, an area with a seemingly endless number of options and choices, can easily become an overwhelming experience. You need clarity to develop a plan of attack that will help you make the best choices for you and your family based on your individual situation. We call this the preparedness prism.

Just as any prism separates the light that pours in from the sun into a brilliant display of color, the Practical Tactical Preparedness Prism helps you bend the glaring and sometimes blinding light that shines from the vast universe of techniques and gear associated with preparedness and separate out the most useful options that best meet the needs of you and your family.

Like a traditional prism, the Practical Tactical Preparedness Prism is made up of three sides…Planning, Purpose of Use and Practice.

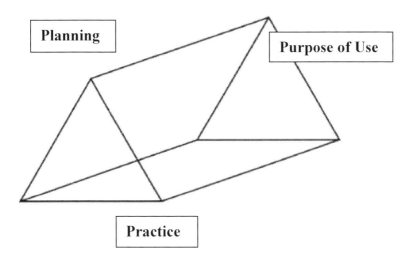

We have already discussed *developing a disaster preparedness plan*. This plan establishes the framework that will guide every decision you make going forward. Now the hard work of figuring out what you need and why you need it to achieve your preparedness goals begins. You should know the *purpose of use* for every tool, skill and piece of gear you add to any of your disaster kits, and the knowledge of what it is, what it's for and how you use it should accompany every item in any kit you build. If it does not, you should consider your kit incomplete.

The third side of our preparedness prism is *practice*. Regardless of whether it is a new plan or a change to an existing one, a new piece of gear or a newly gained skill, you must put it into practice. This is the only verifiable way to determine its practical value.

Taking a look at each preparedness decision through the Practical Tactical Preparedness Prism will lessen the chance of making a bad choice. Because you are doing the great work of planning ahead, you have given yourself the opportunity to reassess and make the right choice before your and your family's lives depend on it.

Another tool we use to refine our planning and decision-making process is the Practical Tactical Preparedness Cycle. This is a process of education and assessment, developing a personalized preparedness plan and then building your kit to fit your plan as opposed to working things the other way around, followed up with training and evaluation. Once you complete your evaluation of how things are working with your current setup, the process starts over again as you take what you have learned and move forward.

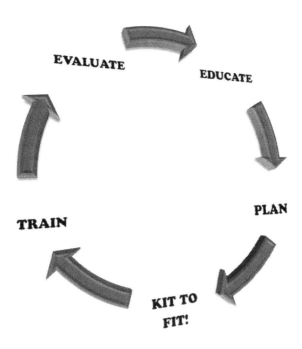

When you look at your situation, develop a plan and start to think about the gear it might take to build out each of your kits, it is going to sound like a lot of stuff, and that can be intimidating. Then there's the cost of getting the gear you need. If you do not make good choices as you go and are forced to learn by trial and error, resulting in buying the same type of gear again and again, this process can get expensive in a hurry. However, this does not have to be a roadblock to your preparedness. Using tools like the Practical Tactical Preparedness Prism and the Preparedness Cycle, you can better identify your needs and make the best choice for your situation the first time, and that will save you both the anxiety of indecision and worry as well as money.

How much you choose to spend on the gear for each of your disaster kits is up to you, just remember it does not have to be a prohibitive factor when choosing your gear. There is not a magic number that will somehow make your gear any better or more reliable when you need it most. However, that is not to say that price never equates to quality. The important thing to remember is you can get reliable gear at an affordable price that will absolutely meet the needs of your disaster plan without breaking the bank. You have to do your research, and you may have to shop around a bit to find what suits your needs, but you can cover your preparedness and still stick to your budget. Every day, we all have to make choices in our daily lives based on our priorities. The same is true in preparedness. The Preparedness Prism and Cycle will help you set those priorities. With this knowledge, you can confidently go out and get the gear that best fits your plan and your budget. With this in mind, it is helpful to remember that when you pay for quality, you usually only have to pay once, and that is important. Assess your situation, develop a plan based on your circumstances, and then go out and get the highest quality gear that you can afford that suits your needs.

In the United States, a person's home is usually their greatest investment. More importantly, it is a place of safety where the memories that will be cherished for a lifetime are made. From a preparedness point of view, a person's primary residence is usually where they keep the majority of their emergency supplies. The idea that we would ever leave our home voluntarily during a disaster is completely foreign to most of us. Most everyone would choose to shelter in place or "bug in" and remain in their homes if given the chance. However, that does not mean we will never face a forced evacuation. Should we ever be forced to pull up stakes and BOLT or "bug out," we must be ready. Using the basic tenets of preparedness as a guide, viewing the many challenges of crafting an effective plan for survival through the Practical Tactical Preparedness Prism, and then testing those plans with the Practical Tactical Preparedness Cycle, you will develop a multitiered preparedness plan for you and your family or group that is practical, resilient and flexible. This process will allow you to build layers of preparedness into your daily life right now and provide you with options should you ever face a disaster situation in the future.

Chapter 6: SHELTER

Kate aligned the rechargeable screwdriver with the barrel hinge, and drove the three-inch stainless steel screws flush with the hardware. She repeated the process for the remaining three screws, handing the screwdriver to Alex, who was situated across the ply board, on a second ladder. Kate kept the board pushed against the window frame, as he adjusted the right hinge, trying to place it level with the other hinge. Over the past two days, the two of them had managed to construct makeshift hurricane shutters for all of the second story windows, depleting most of the ply board supply.

They grabbed the board near the bottom corners and lifted, swinging the heavy board upward and outward. The hinges didn't move as they lowered the board back in place. Crude but effective. The board covered the window, but was far from airtight, with half inch to quarter inch spaces lining the sides. Once the weather turned, they'd have to attach some type of commercial weather stripping—anything to block the cold drafts that would pour through these cracks. One step at a time. For now, they needed the ability to keep the rain from pouring directly into the house. They could refine the process later.

—From *Event Horizon*

Steven

"Mi casa es su casa." Except during a pandemic. That was the hardline stance taken by Alex Fletcher in *The Jakarta Pandemic* to protect the most valuable component of his survival plan—the roof and four walls standing between his family and the outside world.

He made no exceptions, even opting to take the fight to the enemy in the middle of a blizzard to prevent a breach of his enclave. Smart move on his part—does that mean I'm a genius for writing it? Not really. I didn't invent Alex's overriding instinct to protect his home. Humans (and the vast majority of living creatures on planet Earth) have been obsessed with shelter since the dawn of time—for good reason. Shelter satisfies many of our basic human needs. Privacy, security, protection from the elements, comfort and familiarity.

Of course, it's hard to call shopping for a 2,000-square-foot house in the best school district "seeking shelter," but the same core needs apply, with a few added "wants." Most of us live in this world—where we still have the relative luxury of choosing our shelter. It doesn't matter whether you're signing a lease for a two-bedroom apartment, two-car garage bi-level, two-acre farmhouse or a two-million-dollar mansion with a view of the ocean; the feeling is still the same. THIS IS HOME. Unfortunately, this feeling can work against you.

I'm not saying you should trade backyard (or balcony) barbeques for a cardboard sign reading, *"Homeless by Choice! I didn't want to get bogged down with the BARRICADE mindset created by investing time, money and emotion in a fixed location."* The light will change to green before they finish reading the sign. What I'm saying is SHELTER is a complicated topic, which bears some examination. Trust me, I'm not giving up my house any time soon, but I do have a plan in case **I can't stay here**. RULE OF THREES applies—*actually we might be in the RULE OF FIVES because we recognize the critical importance of shelter.* I'm going to list some options we've considered, hoping they'll help frame your family discussion about planning for shelter.

1. Regardless of the disaster, we'd LIKE to stay in the home we built (not by hand—we're not that industrious) and spent the last ten years in as a family. It's going to take one hell of a crisis to push us out of our comfort zone here at the Casa de Konkoly

(Sorry, Hungarian and Spanish words don't sound right together). We're right there with 99% of you. When the SHTF, I'd prefer to wipe down the fan and spray some air freshener. Am I being stubborn? No. Why? Let's go back to the second chapter. SURVIVE WHAT? The most likely disaster scenarios in Maine don't involve hiking out of my neighborhood or driving west. This is simple economy of effort. I'm putting most of my time, effort and resources toward staying in my house. MOST. Options 2-5 reflect the possibility, however slight, that we might have to go on an unplanned "vacation."

2. Whether we drive, bicycle or walk out of here, we have a primary destination (more on that later). I have no problem sleeping in a car or a tent, but if I can swing a hotel room for the family, I'll take that option. I'm just going to assume that cash will be the only form of payment accepted, and make sure we always have enough cash to cover a few hotel stays en route to our "vacation" spot.

3. Most of you know that I own a sailboat. It's a twenty-eight-footer—just big enough to keep us from killing each other if the weather sours during our weeklong family sailing trips. This may sound crazy, but I feel better about our survival options when the boat launches in June. For the span of four months, I have an unfettered way to escape Maine. No traffic jams, zombie hoards, angry neighbors, just a rolling blue highway to any destination along the East Coast—even another continent. Maybe you have an RV or something similar to consider. Disclaimer: I didn't just tell you to drive your RV into the ocean.

4. Tenting is fun! Said nobody after the seventh day in a tent, under any circumstances. Hotels won't always be an option while travelling, and in some cases, you might not want to get close enough to populations centers to make them an option. We keep a larger tent with our "Car Kit" and smaller tents or shelter materials (tarp) within our individual BOLT kits. Tents can serve as temporary shelters on the way to a secondary location, or they

might become your semipermanent shelter—in some climate zones they can be used as permanent shelter. Tents give you a ton of flexibility, and guess what? A tent is one of the few major items in your overall survival kit that can be used outside of the apocalypse—to have fun! Camping. All this talk about doom and gloom, and you still get to enjoy yourself. Who would have thought that?

5. Everyone gather around. I have a secret to tell you, and I don't want the word reaching my brother-in-law—yet. He might get a visit from us if the SHTF. Nothing confirmed. Just thinking out loud. But it sure would be nice to have a place in the mountains, with people I trust, when society collapses. Probably not going to happen, but if it did, we might be headed to Vermont. 188 miles—not that I've used Google Maps to measure the distance.

6. Don't feel like sharing space with the in-laws? Buy your own Bug Out Location (BOL). I put this last on the list, because it's by far the most expensive and complicated option. Some of you might have a cottage, lake house, rural property, or camp (that's what they call a summer home in Maine) that can serve as the family BOL. I'm not talking about a cottage on the busiest lake in New Hampshire. You don't want to trade a busy spot in the suburbs, where people might have their own supplies, for a busy spot on a lake where a two-day supply of Doritos, hot dogs, condiments and toilet paper summarizes most vacationer's readiness standards (off-season might work). I think we'll circle back to Bug Out Locations in Chapter 20: Should I Stay or Should I Go.

Randall

As we mentioned in the last chapter, shelter is one of the basic tenets of preparedness. Regardless of the disaster situation you find yourself in, how you take shelter from the elements is a need that must be addressed. If you are fortunate enough to be able to remain in your home or some other place you are intimately familiar with during a disaster, this problem is solved. Every one of us would take this option if it were available to us. Not only is our home where we are most comfortable both physically and psychologically, it is where we have every tactical advantage. Whether it is the availability of supplies or knowledge of the surrounding area and the people in it, when it comes to shelter, you could not be in a more advantageous circumstance for survival.

Given that you have the advantage of being able to shelter at home during a disaster, you have the ability to take extra measures to improve your situation. You can spend the time you would have spent squaring away your shelter on other preparedness considerations like addressing any of the other basic tenets of preparedness, fortifying your home's defenses or spending some time helping others in your family or group or in your community.

Should disaster strike when you are not at home or if you are forced to evacuate in an emergency situation, the issue of shelter quickly becomes paramount and must be dealt with. Whether it is your BOLT kit, a get-home bag or your everyday carry, each of your mobile kits should have multiple options for emergency shelter built into them depending on the corresponding plan for each kit. For instance, in a BOLT kit you may have a small camping tent, a tarp and an emergency blanket. In a get-home bag, you may have opted for a bivvy (bivouac) sack, a small tarp and a waterproof rain shell, whereas in your everyday carry kit, you carry an emergency blanket, a quality poncho and a few heavy-duty trash bags. Remember to take seasonal weather patterns for your area into consideration when building out your mobile kits and adjust the corresponding gear in each kit as necessary, keeping a wary eye on rapidly changing weather conditions.

Earlier this year, I lived a prime example of an emergency situation developing while you're away from home and what can happen when you're not prepared….and what can happen when you are. In late January of 2014 the city of Atlanta, along with much of the Deep South, was brought to its collective knees by a major winter storm. What follows is a post from the Practical Tactical blog that chronicles the events that followed.

FROZEN: The 2014 Atlanta Ice Emergency

I am quite certain you have heard about a small weather situation that has unfolded across the Deep South over the last twenty-four-plus hours or so. What looked like a winter storm that would bring some frozen precipitation to the region as it skirted along the gulf coast and southern third of the eastern seaboard wiggled to the north just a bit and exploded into a nightmare, worst-case scenario, and the "fun" began. Everything came together in a pure symphony of suck to unleash stress, fear and danger on the South's hospitable population.

Despite the best efforts of our local leadership to convince everyone they had learned the lessons from the 2011 Snowpocalypse that shut down the city of Atlanta for the better part of a week and that all of the appropriate adjustments had been made, this weather event….a full three years hence….laid bare these very dangerous truths:

*There were government failures at every level to assess the threat and properly deploy assets in advance of the storm

*Poor decisions by Georgia DOT resulted in a failure to sufficiently treat roadways prior to the weather event

*Poor transportation infrastructure that has elevated ramps, bridges and inclines everywhere exacerbate any inclement weather issue

Now, some thirty-six hours later, it is clear that the hard lessons taught in the 2011 storm were not learned by this local and state government at all. Even with new plans in place and some new equipment at their disposal, the end result was not better in 2014 than it was in 2011. In fact, in many ways, it was worse.

All of the key players were telling us right up until the snow started to fall that there were plans in place and that this time things would be better. "Don't worry about anything, John Q. We've got it covered. Everything will be fine." More trucks. New plans. And, by the way, everyone just "stay off the roads." Well, it quickly became apparent that the only way any of these extra trucks or new plans were going to make any difference at all was if everyone actually did stay off the roads. And that would be impossible. Wait, did I mention that there were no closures of government offices or metro schools in advance of the storm? No? And what about the fact that businesses certainly were not shuttering for the day? No? Oh, well then. Here's the best part. The same people that were telling everyone to stay off the roads...remember that's the underlying key to the entire plan...those same people issued a statement just before the inclement weather began telling everyone to get out of downtown, leave work now and go home. In other words, just as the storm was kicking up it was like they said, "Everyone! Get on the roads riiiiiiiiiiight...NOW!"

And that's when the apocalypse porn visuals started streaming out of Atlanta.

Unlike the decision makers for the state of Georgia and the city of Atlanta, I, my wife, all my friends and virtually everyone with a weather app on their smartphone or an internet connection or a television or radio knew that the city of Atlanta was going to get hit with about two inches of snow with some ice thrown in for good measure. It didn't take a meteorologist (by the way, my cousin is a meteorologist) to figure this one out, folks. So, with this info in my back pocket, I set out to get a plan to deal with the issues that I believed were sure to arise since I was scheduled to head to work for an evening shift (in the center of downtown Atlanta) Tuesday afternoon right as the storm was getting started.

I have a forty-five-mile commute to work, so I don't leave the house without a plan on a perfectly normal day and the gear to fit it. But when there's a 100% chance of accumulating winter precipitation in a city where that don't usually happen, you better believe I am coming prepared and loaded for bear. So, I headed into work with everything I would need to spend the night rather than taking the risk of getting back out on what I was quite certain would be a skating rink in the wee hours of the morning. Of course, I had my Every Day Carry (EDC) with me and my Get Home Bag (GHB) in the back of my vehicle as I always do, but on this day I also loaded up the sleep gear I take when I go camping, about three times the normal amount of food I would carry on my person, and I tossed my BOLT kit in the back of the truck just to cover all the bases.

So I hit the road with the flakes a-flyin', and sure enough, a ride that usually takes me about fifty minutes took three hours. During my travels, I watched as the major interstates and surface streets were already glazing over with ice. I dodged travelers that were spinning out left and right as I made my way to work, finally headed inside to watch the frozen drama unfold.

During the evening, I had several coworkers decide to take their chances with the weather and try for home. Around 7 pm, a friend that travels a route similar to mine decided to strike out for home. Five hours later, he called in to let us know he was sitting on I-85 (only about fifteen miles from our building), stuck in traffic, and that he hadn't moved at all in about three hours. He had no food, no water, no blankets or anything to keep warm with him in the vehicle and no hope of moving any time soon. Right about now I was feeling awful for my pal, but pretty good about my preparations and my plan to stay put.

At the end of my shift, I posted the following status update on Facebook to let my family and friends know what was going on with me:

"Ah, weekend. Hello again, old friend. I can't wait to get home and…oh, that's right. I can't go anywhere. I'm encased in ice and miles from home. Very thankful right now to know that the homestead is safe and secure in all ways even though I can't be there. Anyways, tomorrow brings the sun (even with tough temps), and that presents my next opportunity to get home. Take care all."

I walked out to my vehicle and grabbed my gear for the evening. Even from street level, I could see the city was absolutely crystallized in ice. I paired up with a couple of my coworkers that had also decided to stay, and we settled in for the night, watching television in astonishment as thousands of people were sitting in vehicles on seemingly every major roadway surrounding the city with zero chance of going anywhere any time soon. Not to mention all of the children around the city and across the region that were stuck in schools, where they would have to spend the night, or on the roads in buses that would not be heading home on this bitter night. That part was unimaginable.

Upon waking we learned that the roads were still locked up with some people now approaching twenty-five-plus hours stranded in their vehicles. Parents with young children stuck on the road with no food and no water. How does that happen? I can't imagine being in that scenario on a perfect day, much less one that everyone should have known was going to turn out like this one had. People running out of gas, ditching vehicles and being forced to walk to safe havens just to escape the brutal weather only to end up sleeping in the aisles of a grocery or convenience store. On the bright side, we did learn that our friend that had been stuck on I-85 had finally made it home safely around 5 am that morning. When I checked my phone for the first time, I saw that my wife had posted this status update on Facebook:

"Anyone that was stranded in Atlanta's epic fail of 2014, I hope you will be able to make it home soon. If you aren't prepared to take care of yourself, you are s.o.l. because no one is coming to help you. That seems to be the lesson learned by Atlanta on this day. Don't laugh at people who prep, they plan for the worst and hope for the best. The worst happened in Atlanta yesterday. Be prepared, people."

What can I say? That's awesome.

Even in this awful situation there were some bright spots that make me very proud of the people that live and work in the great state of Georgia and of humanity in general. Stories of people walking right down the middle of six-lane interstates that were eerily at a standstill, handing out water and food to those people that had been stranded for hours, travelers helping one another to get vehicles unstuck and moving once again, and even the glorious news of a child named Grace being born in a stranded vehicle that was stuck in traffic on I-285, the perimeter highway that rings Atlanta.

After packing all my gear and checking to see if I could help any of my coworkers, I headed for home. Because I'm fortunate enough to have people near and far that care about me and pray for my safety that knew I was getting underway, I shared the following status update when I arrived home:

"So, this January's weather experience has come to a gratifying end for me. I left work at 11:30 this morning and rolled into the house about 12:30 pm, which is really pretty good. Upon arrival I found the homestead warm and welcoming with my loving wife and two adoring pups thrilled to see me, a roaring fire and a pot of hot coffee beckoning. Last night was as good as it could be given the situation, and the company certainly didn't hurt. The best part of this story is that I didn't spend one moment in fret or worry, either for myself or Alice, because we had taken the time to plan for the worst eventualities and made the appropriate preparations ahead of the emergency. Although the weather forced us to be apart, she knew I would be okay, and I knew that she would be safe, warm and happy. All of this thanks to a little foresight and taking the action steps necessary to insure such an outcome. Thanks to everyone that offered thoughts or voiced support and wishes of well-being. I appreciate each and every one of those actions and each and every one of you."

For the second time in a handful of years the city of Atlanta and my beloved home state of Georgia have been in the nation's spotlight thanks to paralysis due to a winter weather emergency. So much danger, human distress and property damage on display for the world to see, and it really saddens me. It makes me sad because I know that so much of it can be avoided altogether with just a little planning and forethought, both on an individual and a governmental scale. These people don't have to suffer like they have. All of these lives don't have to be put at risk. These situations could be mostly prevented if only there were better overall planning put in place by those that are supposed to lead, and each individual made their personal security during the situations their top priority. On the other side of the coin, my experience was as safe, warm and as comfortable as it could have possibly been.

There were those behind the power curve with no plan and no preparations that found themselves caught up in the chaos because they were waiting on someone else to tell them what to do, and then you have the example I try to live out where you get a plan, build a kit to fit, and execute a plan of action to the best of your ability based on sound information you have gleaned ahead of time. Which one would you choose?

It really is so easy to take the necessary steps and get this done so that you and your family won't be caught in the whirlwind the next time it blows. Here's hoping you will choose to do so.

Semper Paratus!

How you choose to outfit your various kits is up to you, but don't lock yourself into one idea of what shelter can be. A useful shelter can be virtually anything as long as it effectively gets you out of the elements. Remembering to keep your options open and remaining flexible is the key, especially with your mobile kits. If you're on the move, whether trying to get back home or just going from point A to point B, the concept of "mobile shelter" is something that can be advantageous to you. What is "mobile shelter," you ask? Well, preparedness friends, it's really straightforward, and I'm betting you're more familiar with the concept than you may realize. "Mobile shelter" is anything that gives you shelter from the elements that allows you to remain on the move. Umbrella, anyone? I know, I know…and I hear you. You're trying to make it home during an emergency, not taking a stroll through the park. But the idea is the same. An umbrella isn't exactly the kind of shelter you might have had in mind, but in a pinch it would get the job done. Other, more "tactical" options are the types of items I mentioned above. A waterproof rain jacket, a heavy poncho, a tarp or an emergency blanket are all things that you could use to shelter yourself and your other gear from the elements that are lightweight, packable and would allow you to continue towards your destination.

If you are attempting to make your way home during an emergency, the first thing you must know is that the landscape you will have to navigate will be wholly different than your normal daily commute. Now I'm not saying there will be a series of checkpoints dotting your usual route home that restricts movement in and out of the city or that you will be dealing with boots on the ground under martial law, but odds are there will be an unsettling chaos bubbling just under the surface, and at the very least your fellow citizens will be just as anxious, possibly frightened, and as on edge as you are. This is a potentially dangerous convergence of circumstances. If self-preservation is an instinct you possess, stealth, avoidance and a general notion to mind your own *@%! business is always a good idea when moving in an emergency situation. You're on a mission, and you may have people depending on the success of that mission waiting for you at the end of your journey. You cannot afford to take too many chances.

Given the climate of the situation you will be facing, keeping your head down and staying away from crowds will probably be a good idea. This will force you to slow down or possibly take an alternate route, and you could find yourself somewhere between points A and B when the night (or the weather) comes in, and you will need to find shelter. Depending on how you have chosen to build out your kit, you may not have a "traditional" overnight shelter setup with you. You may be able to stay dry, but you should always be looking to improve your situation when it comes to an element of survival as important as shelter. This is where creating a shelter or utilizing a "found" shelter will serve you well. Using the gear you have in your kit, like a cutting tool and cordage, along with items you may be able to scavenge in an urban environment or the surrounding natural resources afforded you in a more rural setting, you can build a more primitive type shelter like a lean-to, a wickiup or a debris shelter to get you through the night. You can also use existing structures as an emergency overnight shelter. Whether it's an overpass or an overhanging rock ledge, sheltering in locations where the work of creation has already been done for you is always a smart move in a survival situation.

The bottom line is that having a way to shelter in a disaster or emergency situation is a must, regardless of whether you are in your home or on the move. Using the preparedness prism and the kit to fit concept as a guide, you can address one of your basic preparedness needs and build resilience into each of your kits by identifying what you need to accomplish based on your disaster plan, selecting the appropriate gear and scaling that gear up or down to fit the needs of each kit.

In the world of preparedness, it is often said that the time to repair the roof is when the sun is shining, and that is especially true when the preparedness topic of discussion is shelter. Get your shelter setup squared away now while the sun is still shining to make sure that you and your family or group can weather the storm when it comes.

Chapter 7: WATER

"You swam across the Charles at night, with all of this gear?"

"I told you he was a mercenary," said someone.

"Believe whatever you want. I don't really give a shit. I'm leaving, and nobody is following. I'll leave a water filter behind for you. It's a hand-pumped type, good for five hundred gallons. You can catch rainwater in the trashcans or fetch water from the river. Whatever you do, don't let anyone see it, or you'll have a fight on your hands."

—From *Event Horizon*

He decided to start at the wall adjacent to the door. The metal storage shelves started there and extended to the front concrete wall of the basement and contained spring water in two-gallon containers. Each four-level shelving unit held thirty of these containers, all on the lowest three shelves. The containers were stacked five in a row, two rows high on each shelf. There were eight shelving units along this wall, together holding nearly five hundred gallons of water.

All of the containers were marked with their date of purchase. Each week, at least one of the oldest containers was removed and placed in the kitchen for consumption. During the weekly grocery run, the container would be replaced, ensuring that the water supply stored in the basement was slowly turned over throughout the course of the year, preventing the inevitable decay of the plastic containers.

—From *The Jakarta Pandemic*

Randall

When it comes to water, there are no two ways about it. You've got to have it. It doesn't matter if we're talking about your home, your community or society as a whole. Without water, everything simply stops. In the United States access to fresh water has been so effortless for so long that for the general public, it's like breathing. We use this most precious resource without even thinking about it. We are used to taking long hot showers, sometimes more than once a day, just because it feels good. We would quickly gain a different perspective if we were forced to haul gallons of water up from the lake or river and then purify it simply to complete everyday tasks. Fresh and clean water for drinking, food preparation and hygiene all right at our fingertips, it just flows from the tap like magic. It really is a small miracle.

Because we really don't have to think about water in America, most people have no idea of how it gets to their tap. Unless operating on a completely gravity-fed system, and there are very few of those across our country, municipalities are forced to pump water through the system. It takes a very complex and interdependent collection of systems to make this small miracle that we know as our municipal water system a reality. It takes electricity to run those pumps and miles and miles of (often aging) pipeline infrastructure to deliver that water to your home. The more complex a system is, the more opportunities there are for it to suffer a critical failure that would leave your home, your neighborhood or your city high and dry. From the intake point at the reservoir or river to the water treatment facility to the sewer system to the faucets in your home, there are a thousand points along the way at which your access to fresh and clean water can be interrupted due to environmental pollution or depletion, infrastructure failure or terrorist threat. It doesn't even take a disaster to force a disruption in service for your home or community. If major water delivery infrastructure maintenance is required, your entire neighborhood or business district could be left without water for days or weeks.

In parts of the American southwest and from California to Texas, up through the Great Plains region known as America's Breadbasket, the issue of fresh water is already becoming a daily topic of discussion and concern for many. There are a myriad of reasons for this concern, and each is justified. From years of severe drought to simply having too many "straws in the milkshake" upriver, communities across the region are struggling to meet their water needs. Faced with ever-growing demand, local governments are beginning to take increasingly drastic measures to keep pace. Hundreds of millions of dollars are being spent on new water treatment facilities like the huge desalinization plant under construction in Carlsbad, California. In California's Orange County, the wastewater treatment facility that recycles sewage and returns it to the community's drinking supply is expanding production from seventy to one hundred million gallons per day. That's right, straight from toilet to tap. Similar initiatives are being launched at great expense in Los Angeles, San Francisco, San Diego, as well as in Texas. These technological advances will help meet water needs for the local communities, but they also add new layers of complexity to an already complex system, and complex systems are extremely fragile.

Necessity, vulnerability and availability are all hard facts of life that must be addressed when it comes to the way we maintain and deliver clean water in America. Recognizing that clean water is the foundation of our society, that the method of delivery of that water to our expansive communities is extremely fragile and subject to disruption, and that we as members of the global community are facing a water crisis in just a few short years should provide more than enough motivation for you to want to get a better handle on your personal situation when it comes to such a precious resource.

You can get this done a number of different ways, and that process doesn't have to be a difficult one. At a bare minimum, you should store at least one gallon of water per person per day to cover your basic drinking, cooking and hygiene needs. A normally active person needs at least one gallon of water daily just for drinking, so you may want to consider storing a second gallon per person per day to cover sanitation and other needs. Individual needs vary, depending on age, physical condition, activity, medical conditions, diet and climate, so be certain to factor in all of the variables for your situation.

There are options for water like private wells that are self-contained and have the ability to be completely off the grid with the right setup, but that is not an option for most of us. However, that doesn't mean we're up a creek without a paddle.

You can easily store enough water to get you through most disaster situations. Water is heavy, and it takes up a lot of space, but you have several options at your disposal that you can use to meet the requirements of your preparedness plan. Bottled water is always an option. You can buy the prepackaged options or bottle your own for storage, just remember to rotate your stored water regularly. If you choose to bottle your own water from the tap, avoid containers like milk jugs, which are difficult to clean properly, and stick to the hard plastic options like empty soda bottles. Make sure to follow all water treatment protocols when storing your own water.

If you don't have a lot of room in your home (or even if you do), you may want to consider harvesting water by installing a rain-catchment system outside your home. This is a very efficient way of collecting large amounts of clean water rapidly. Your rain-harvesting system can be as large as you want it to be and can be put together with little effort and at very small cost. This water can then be used for everything from meeting your basic needs to serving as a water source for your animals or any gardening you may be doing. This is a large part of my personal water preparedness plan for my home. We did a little research online and found a couple of used cisterns at a local business. Each cistern is made with food-grade plastic, holds two hundred fifty gallons and has a large and very solid ball valve. I was able to buy these used containers at what I considered to be a steal of a price. After a quick trip to my local home warehouse store and about an hour of installation time, we had built our very own five-hundred-gallon rain-catchment system. To give you an idea of just how efficient this system is for us, given the square footage of the area of my roof that empties into the gutter that flows into our cisterns, it only takes about an inch of rainfall to fill one of the two-hundred-fifty-gallon containers to overflowing. That's not too bad at all.

You also have options for water storage that you can deploy at the last minute if a possible emergency situation is imminent, such as filling bath tubs and sinks from the tap. Even if you already have stored water in your home, this is still an appealing option that will add to your total water storage. If you choose to build this method of water storage into your plan, you may want to consider that there are bladder options that connect to your faucet and fit inside your bathtub out there that are relatively inexpensive (around $20) and are quite popular. After disaster strikes and water service is disrupted or if there is any risk that your municipal water system has been contaminated and you are forced to shut off the water to your home at the main valve, you can still find clean water in your home by draining the pipes inside your house. The water inside your water heater is also considered a safe source of drinking water. Of course, if you have any reservations as to the quality of water, you should take steps to make it safe before use.

Conservation should always be a top consideration when dealing with water in a disaster situation. This does not mean that you should ration water! People should always be allowed to drink according to their needs. Just take common sense steps like not flushing toilets and taking sponge baths instead of tub baths. Simply taking basic steps like these will save dozens of gallons of water, thus providing you with a tactical preparedness advantage.

If the water stops flowing from your tap, you will need to find another source of water. We've already discussed a couple of ways you can utilize stored water to get through a municipal water service disruption, but that should not be the end of your planning. Odds are there is at least one natural water source like a pond, lake or river near your location, and you should know where it is located. Unless it is on your property and very close to your home, you should not count this as your primary water source in a disaster situation simply based on the logistics of transporting that water to your home. However, knowing where this "wild" water source is could prove to be a valuable piece of information should a disaster situation deteriorate and/or turn into a longer term survival scenario. When considering this possibility, it is beneficial to recognize that there are several methods available to you that can be used to locate "wild" water sources or even create your own fresh water such as building a solar still. This is not a bushcraft guide or a primitive survival skills how-to manual so I will not attempt to identify them all or go into the details of each. Just know that this is a set of skills that you can acquire should you choose to add it to your preparedness toolbox.

With that said, there are basic methods of water purification that we absolutely recommend when it comes to dealing with found water that are both practical and can be scaled to meet your needs. You can boil it, you can treat it with chemicals, or you can filter it. Each of these methods will render found water biologically safe.

The ability to boil water as a purification technique is a winner because it's versatile. Whether you're at home or on the move, if you can build a fire, you can have safe water to drink. When it comes to versatility, treating water chemically is another go-to move. You can add purification tablets or even a small bottle of bleach (use in the appropriate amounts) to any disaster kit, home or mobile, and you will be good to go. A simpler option, although a more costly one, is a quality water filter. Many of us already filter the water that comes into our homes. I have a filter on the back of my refrigerator that filters the water for my ice maker, another mounted to the kitchen faucet and yet another that's built into a pitcher that lives inside the fridge! None of these purchases forced me to forego my favorite coffee the last time I was at Starbucks, and I'm glad we have them. Speaking of coffee, without water there can be no coffee. Can you imagine trying to survive the end of the world as we know it without good coffee? Now THAT would be a real disaster. There are much larger and more expensive gravity-fed water filtration options available for your home that are very efficient and effective, and they provide an extra layer of protection since they do not require electricity to function, but they come at a much higher cost. Just be sure to do your research before taking the plunge.

We do not live and disaster does not strike in an Etch-A-Sketch world. We can't always take a straight line from here to there. Having safe water to drink when you're on the go in an emergency situation is a must, and you just never know where you might find yourself when you're in need of a sip. That's why the preparedness universe gave us the backpacker-style water filter. This nifty little invention comes in all shapes, sizes and filtration methods...and price points. Whether you opt for a top-of-the-line backcountry water filter or something as simple as a LifeStraw, having a filtration option that you can count on when you're away from home can be a life saver....literally. Of course, you can always choose to carry water, but that wouldn't be my first choice. Bladder systems like CamelBak and others are useful and very good at what they are intended to do. If you're constantly on the go and need to keep your hands free, bladder systems are great. Canteens and water bottles will certainly get the job done too, but both systems have limits in the bigger picture. For one, water is heavy and cumbersome to carry around. Also, these systems have a limited capacity, which means you will have to refill them eventually anyway, so why not go ahead and cut out the middle man by carrying a water filter. Do you have to? No, but it is a very practical option.

Water is life. When it comes to preparedness, access to clean water is not negotiable. When your world has been thrown into a state of chaos, opening yourself up to the possibility of contracting deadly waterborne diseases such as cholera and diarrhea is not a very appealing option and can be easily avoided. By taking practical steps to strengthen your water resilience today, you won't have to worry the next time you open your faucet and nothing happens...whatever the reason.

Steven

I drink too much water during the day. That's a good problem to have. Ever go without water or your favorite beverage for longer than you're accustomed? In my case that's a little more than an hour. You start to get a little panicky, or maybe a little testy if it's a caffeine-based drink. Let's take it a step further. Have you ever been a situation where you absolutely couldn't get water or a refreshing Coolatta when you wanted it? You suddenly become the poster child for entitled Westerners. What? You don't have any more bottled water? What about tap water? Is it filtered? What do you mean I have to buy a bag of chips or a sandwich to get a plastic cup for tap water? %$#& that! Crashing through the door into the sweltering 81-degree heat of Boston's North End, you wonder how in the hell you're going to hydrate yourself?

That last vignette was designed to make you smile. It's ridiculous, but at the same time, we've all been there to some degree. I know I have. It's particularly outlandish because we don't have a real water crisis in America, regardless of what you hear about California. Water still flows out of the taps. We may be on the way toward an economic crisis caused by declining water tables in the Midwest and Southwest, but nobody envisions a day when the taps stop flowing. Sadly enough, the tap doesn't flow for nearly 1.2 billion people in the world. I'm willing to bet this group wouldn't have a problem "hydrating" in one of Boston's busiest restaurant districts on a day that felt like air-conditioning to them.

Fortunately, we don't have this problem—YET. Do I know something you don't know? Of course not, but I do know that water is always one of the most difficult resources to procure in a natural disaster, and we have plenty of natural disasters in the United States. In the aftermath of Hurricane Katrina, the lack of available drinking water persisted as a major problem long after the tidal waters receded. Water seems to hide during a crisis, even though we can find it everywhere. We've become so reliant on the kitchen sink or backyard garden hose—***that many of us don't know where to get fresh water outside of the house or a store.*** By the way, does anyone drink out of a garden hose anymore? Case in point.

All right, if you live on a lake or next to a river, I take back what I just said. You're probably savvy enough to unravel the water mystery, as long as you purify the water first. I don't care how clean it looks, Bob just went "number two" through the hole he cut in his dock, because he got tired of filling the toilet tank with water from the lake. Never assume water is safe to drink in a disaster, even from the faucet.

For those of us without the luxury of an unlimited supply of "brown water," I pose this question: ***Where would you get your water if the something knocked out the public water supply, killed the power to your well pump, or you had to leave your house?*** It's a scary thought, especially when you need at least one gallon of water a day, just for consumption. That's assuming a regular level of activity. If you're bugging out on foot, that number could double or triple. You can get away with less, but sooner or later, you have to bring water consumption levels up to par.

Whenever our kids push their food around at the dinner table and I tell them to eat because there are starving children in Africa (I like the Africa theme), my wife says the same thing. "Honey, they're fine. It takes three to four weeks to die of starvation." That's a fact I didn't know, and she's right. The kids will be fine. They won't be fine if they stop drinking water. You can die of dehydration within three to five days depending on your health and physical exertion levels. Water is critical, and my family has a layered approach to staying "hydrated" during a disaster. Looks like I'm going the list route again.

1. We keep containers of water in the house, similar to the Fletchers. Mostly the two-gallon rectangular jugs produced by our local purveyor of spring water. This strategy serves two purposes. First, it gives us an immediate, no-hassle source of water, in the event that something knocks out the water distribution system or we suspect the system to be compromised (purification plant sabotaged or maybe Bob decided to take his business to the nearest pump station). Second, it's portable—sort of. Two gallons weighs sixteen pounds. You're not hiking out with one in each hand unless you're crossing the street. I keep eight of these in the garage to throw in the car if we have to make a quick getaway. That's four days of water. Plenty of time to put other options into play.

2. Another popular option (among preppers) is to rig large, food-grade plastic drums to catch and store rainwater. This is a nice, long-term solution if you can stay at your house. Most of the

systems are designed to capture water from rain gutters. It doesn't get any simpler than this. Just make sure to purify the water. Birds spend a lot of time on your roof, and they aren't there to admire your landscaping.

3. Before I talk about portable options, here's one more gem for the house. The "waterBOB." Look it up online. Don't laugh. I know we've talked about Bob, but this guy is different. For less than $20, you can fill your bathtub or any bin with up to a hundred gallons of water. It's a BPA-free, FDA-approved plastic bag (with pump) that fills to the shape of the container. You lay the bag in the tub, attach it to the faucet, and your tub is now a fresh water storage tank. It beats filling up 378 reclaimed two-liter soda bottles (same as one hundred gallons)—**not that you should leave any containers empty in a major crisis.** That's the moral of this option. Keep plenty of containers on hand to fill with water.

4. If you have to leave the comfort of your "waterBOB" haven, your water-carrying options drastically shrink. Driving gives you the ability to carry the most water, as much as you're willing to stuff in your car. I can't imagine loading up more than thirty to forty two-gallon jugs. Maybe you can. I'll leave this up to you. That's not a bad supply of water. If your car stays functional, you're in good shape to reach your destination, unless you're bugging out to Alaska from Maine.

As a pedestrian, I think you're limited to one gallon loaded in a combination of hydration bladders. We have a CamelBak for each member of the family. The adults carry the hundred-ounce version (three liters—less than a gallon) and the kids carry the seventy-ouncers (two liters). That's less water than we'd need in a single day. I have a few extra water bladders, giving us another six liters. Bottom line: We'd need to find water on the first day, bringing me to option 5.

5. Hiking out, you need a way to procure safe water from multiple sources. I don't recommend knocking on doors to refill your CamelBak or sneaking into backyards to drink out of a hose.

If the cooties from the hose don't kill you, the "double-ought" buckshot from a scared homeowner might. A great solution to this problem is a portable water filter. You can find a filter/purifier made by a trusted name like Katadyn or MSR for less than $100. Replacement filters (for another five hundred gallons of drinkable water) cost $10. Too steep? Water purification tablets ($10-15) by the same companies work fine…just bring a strainer to remove all of the "sinkers and floaters" from the pond.

6. Is a sailboat part of your bug out plan? Or do you live near the ocean and want to go absolutely crazy? You can buy a manual desalinator for $1200. Sounds steep, but imagine a life by the sea. Plenty of fish, seaweed (you can eat most of it) and, for the first time ever on the beach, fresh water. Tempting.

7. What else? Some of you are screaming at me. I have a well! Then you are the big winner, as long as you can keep the pump running without grid electricity or have a way to pump the water out manually.

Last thought: My water discussion is more or less limited to consumption needs. When you add cooking and sanitation to the equation, you add roughly one more gallon per person per day. I pray to the faucet gods every day. Please don't stop giving me water!

Chapter 8: FOOD

"Where would we go—Charlie's?"

"I don't think that would work out," he whispered.

"I can't believe someone ransacked all of his stuff," she said.

"It wouldn't have made a difference. He had a year's worth of dehydrated food for four people. We have seventeen mouths to feed. That's three months of minimal rations. Not that it matters."

"We can bring enough food to get us through to the summer," she said.

"Then what? We'd have to start from scratch growing food. It's taken us three years to get to this point, and it's not enough to keep us from digging into the reserve supplies by January. Earlier with this many people. We're barely sustainable for the long run if everyone stays."

—From *Point of Crisis*

The bunker resembled an expanded version of Kate and Alex's Scarborough home. The far western wall, underneath the expanded great room, housed the furnace, hot water tank, oil tanks and electrical system. Sturdy metal shelves lined the rest of the cement foundation, containing enough food and essential supplies to support the Fletchers' core family for at least five years—well beyond the expiration dates on some of the canned goods rotated through the stockpile.

Supplementing the vast selection of canned, pickled and dry goods, a deep tower of pre-packed plastic buckets, each containing one hundred twenty individually sealed freeze-dried meals, occupied the entire wall next to the door. She knew that the buckets alone contained enough meals to sustain eight adults for an entire *year, only requiring water to reconstitute. With a shelf life of twenty-five years, the buckets represented their last option. She shuddered to think how they might feel after eating nothing but freeze-dried food for a year, but it easily beat the alternative.*

—From *Event Horizon*

Steven

One of my favorite lunchtime topics is "what are we having for dinner?" I'm always looking one or two meals ahead. I bet some of you think I'm about to embark on a guilt trip about people in the world (probably in Africa) that don't know when they'll eat their next meal. I don't have to. You know what it's like to feel hungry, and it's not an enjoyable sensation. Oddly enough, I get crankier about food than water. By all logic, it should be the other way around, but it isn't. My kids never throw a fit because they're thirsty. If we run out of snacks (for eating between meals), watch out! Rough seas ahead.

Food serves two purposes. Nourishment and morale. Like my wife said, it takes three to four weeks to die of starvation—from a strictly nutritional perspective. You'll mentally collapse a lot sooner than that, especially in a crisis situation, when everyone is already stressed to maximum levels. Food procurement needs to be a major component of your personal preparedness plan.

There are so many ways to approach this topic. Almost too many to list. Your first instinct might be to plunk down the credit card and buy a year's worth of dehydrated food in the handy tan or white buckets you see on survival/preparedness supply websites. If you have $7,000 burning a hole in your pocket, unlike most of us, you could do way worse. Then again, if your SURVIVE WHAT scenario falls along the continuum of natural disasters, you could probably spread that cash out a little better to cover every topic in this book. Ultimately, it's up to you. Before you press "buy," let's talk about the buckets a little more.

There's no doubt in my mind that these make a fantastic emergency food item. The packets last forever (twenty to twenty-five years), they're easy to transport (throw the bucket in your car or take out packets and stuff them in your pack), and they provide a nice variety. Having two of these buckets (combine an entrée with a vegetable/side dish bucket) can vastly enhance your bug out plan. Here's the catch (a few), as far as I can tell. First, you need to boil water (one to two cups per packet) to reconstitute the food. Make sure you bring a small camping stove with you on the move. Second, the buckets typically hold sixty servings. Each serving represents 250–300 calories. I'm not saying you need to maintain Cracker Barrel-level serving sizes through the apocalypse, but I think it's fair to say that most of us would cry in our sleep if we ate less than a thousand calories a day, especially if we were hiking under stress. If you do the math, each person will need about four servings per day. For a family of four, each bucket will last about four days—just to stem the tears.

Why do I keep railing on these buckets when I truly do think they're important to have on hand? Because I'm afraid too many of us (me included) think if we press "buy," we're covered and we're done. How many of you have a camping stove and enough propane to boil water for the duration of those buckets? That's just one of the questions that I didn't think of at the beginning. It made me think twice about putting all of my eggs in one basket. The food aspect of emergency preparedness is a three-dimensional puzzle best handled by the RULE OF THREES.

If your most likely SURVIVE WHAT scenario keeps you in place, the bulk of your food preparedness work and resources should go to a multilayer approach around your home. For me, that means a storage area containing lots of dried foods (beans, rice and pasta stored in airtight containers) and several shelves of canned foods, which we rotate into our regular meals and replace to keep expiration dates at bay. Combined with a continuously stocked pantry and refrigerator (we shop weekly and often overbuy), our on-hand food supply gives me a peace of mind.

A smaller aspect of our long-term self-reliance plan is a summer garden. We're in our third year of planning, and the garden gives us more every year. At this point, you might be saying to yourself, "Damn, that Konkoly guy has this locked down! Garden too? He's set!" Not really. As Randy so kindly pointed out the other day, on average it takes an acre of land to feed a person for a year. My entire lot is a half-acre, and I'm using about a twentieth of that for the garden. With the growing season ending in early October, someone's going to be hungry in November. In Maine, nothing of substance grows again until mid to late June. That's a big gap.

For us, gardening is a way to cut down on our produce bill in the summer, eat amazingly fresh vegetables every night, and learn an essential skill that will come in handy when the lights go out for good. We just need to master the art of capturing seeds at the end of the season. I hear that FEDCO and Johnny Seeds won't be delivering during the apocalypse.

Obviously, you can't take a garden with you on the road. Like water, the amount of food you can carry shrinks drastically if you decide to bug out. Back to the dehydrated food packets and my favorite option: MREs (Meals Ready to Eat). You can pick up a case of MREs on the Internet for $70. I won't go into too many details, but look for the MREs that include the flameless heater. Add a little water and the heater pouch cooks the entrée. Pretty handy when you can't or don't want to start a fire. Each MRE delivers roughly 1200 calories and comes with side dishes, crackers, condiments, a dessert and a juice drink mix. When "Gunny" threw these out of the back of the five-ton truck to the marines, I was right there jumping up and down to get one!

What's the difference between MREs and dehydrated food packets? I'll keep this simple. They're less expensive per calorie. $70 for 14,000 calories vs. $125 for 16,500. And your kids will have more fun. On the flip side, MREs will only last four to five years under normal basement temperatures. The dehydrated food packets can last twenty-five years. I recommend a mix of both to suit your plan.

I left a few things out, which I'm sure Randy will cover. Farm animals and hunting. Neither of us are hunters, so maybe he won't hit that one. Here's what I'll say, and this comes from the mouth of a vegetarian. You'd be crazy not to incorporate it into your disaster preparedness plan. A wise man once said, "There's no such thing as an atheist in a foxhole," and Charlie Thornton (from my books) said, "There's no such thing as a vegetarian in the apocalypse." I'm feeding my family with whatever I can get my hands on.

Last words here. Remember the words SURVIVE WHAT and figure out what's best for YOUR plan, not mine. This is all about you. If you want the Big Kahuna, one-year stack of dehydrated food buckets, go ahead and press the "buy" button—just make sure your significant other knows that it wasn't my fault. I don't want to see any bad reviews for this book saying "Thanks to Konkoly, I now have thirty-six plastic bins of dehydrated food in my house and a delayed retirement!"

Randall

Who's hungry?

Growing up in the South, it would be a drastic understatement for me to say that food is an important part of everyday life. It is so much more than that. Life down here revolves around food. Casual conversations between friends and neighbors inevitably turn to what's for dinner or how your garden is looking this year. It seems a profound improbability that any gathering of more than two people can take place below the Mason-Dixon Line unless food is involved. Even as we pause to give thanks before the meal, the final words of the blessing are most often marked with a resounding, "Now, let's eat!" In the South, food goes with every occasion. Hell, half the time food is the occasion. We are seasoned pros at making the focus of an entire day's effort whatever prized dish is destined to be the star of tonight's menu. Food is a symbol of community around these parts. Whether there's a death in the family or a new addition, you can expect to see more food hauled in by those coming to visit than any two or three families alone could eat. And don't plan on dropping in for a friendly visit without getting your belly full. I have a large extended family with lots of aunts, uncles and cousins. I can't imagine showing up at any one of their doors and not being treated to something delicious to eat, and the invitation would not be posed in the form of a question. It may not always be a full meal, but I can guarantee I won't leave hungry. I mean, I wouldn't want to hurt their feelings, now would I? And that's exactly what I would be doing if I didn't grab a bite while I was there. What can I say? Every conversation goes better with a big ole cathead biscuit and some sweet tea.

I wanted to share all of that with you in hopes of giving you a little perspective. When I think about being prepared, the issue of food is a really big deal. Not only is it a necessary part of any survival equation, it carries the additional weight of representing much more than just the fuel necessary to keep us going. It represents everything we cherish by association, and it flavors the memories that make up the highlight reel of our lives. Both for our physical as well as our mental well-being, food is a box on the preparedness checklist that we've got to get right.

When you think about food and how you might get through a full-blown disaster situation, or any other disruption to our normal food delivery system, you have to start with what you have on hand. What if you had to get by on what is in your pantry right now? In terms of days, how long would it be before you found yourself out of food and in a really bad way? If the number you came up with totals less than two weeks, you need to start work on improving your food storage. The good news is you can get started as soon as the next time you go to the store.

Our government advises that you have enough food on hand for three days. At Practical Tactical, we recommend that you extend that out to have at least two weeks' worth of food on hand **in addition** to the normal supplies you have in your home. The secret here is that this is a goal that is insanely easy to achieve. Each time you go to shop for groceries, simply add an extra couple of cans or boxes or bags of whatever you would buy in a normal week to your cart. "Store what you eat and eat what you store!" is the rule here. There's no need to get adventurous or experimental. In just a few weeks, you will have built a nice little stockpile. What about not using all of this "extra food" before it goes bad? No worries. The food that makes up this initial buildup of emergency food should be the stuff you already eat regularly, and you will be able to simply rotate it into your normal meal plan.

Once you've got a solid foundation of supplies for your emergency food storage, you will want to think about expanding your options by including some dry goods in your plan like rice, various types of beans, and pasta. Some other things to keep in mind at this stage of the process are exactly who you're buying for and whether there are any diet restrictions to consider. If there are children in your family or group, it would be a good idea to make sure to include foods that you know they will eat. If anyone has dietary needs that require special consideration, it is important to factor that into your buying plans as well. Finally, going back to the idea that food is more than just fuel, you may want to include some "comfort" foods in your emergency storage-buying plan. Familiar favorites can do wonders for your attitude. A chocolate bar can go a long way towards turning that frown upside down.

Before you know it, that two-week supply of "emergency food" (that you may have thought was impossible to build) will turn into a one month's supply, then a two months' supply, and then a six months' supply if you keep at it in a consistent manner. How deep you want to build your larder to be is up to you. Just know that whatever your goal, you can get it done.

If you are considering extending your emergency food supply out to a year or more, there are options for that too. A really convenient way to extend the effective range of your stored food is by adding prepackaged dehydrated options to your pantry's roster. With a shelf life of up to twenty-five years on some of the products available in today's market, storing food for six months to a year doesn't seem like such a big deal. Another extremely versatile and practical option that has an extended shelf life is MREs, or meals ready to eat. These are vacuum-packed, individual meals that on average will provide a solid 1200 calories or more per complete serving.

Our family's emergency food storage plan has three tiers: every day, short term and long term. The everyday supply is the food we keep in the kitchen pantry and in the fridge. It covers two to three weeks without any trouble. The short-term supply is the food we keep in our secondary pantry and deep freezer, which consists of canned goods, various dry goods stored in airtight containers, and foods we have "canned" or put up from our garden. This tier of supplies would push our food security out to two to four months. The long-term supply is a mix of everything listed above, plus a combination of MREs and other dehydrated options. This is the food that we would turn to if we were looking at an extended emergency situation lasting six months to a year. To our way of thinking, if we are looking at a disaster that forces us to rely solely on our stored food for a year, then we are talking about a real game-changing type of event, and nothing will ever be the same. If that's the case, we do not think it's practical for us to store enough food to live on indefinitely, and we had better have other options in place.

Did you notice that I mentioned something about "canned" foods that had come from our garden? I casually slipped that mention in there, but it is actually a huge part of our food-storage plan. As nice as it is to have those dehydrated and prepackaged items available as options for your long-term food storage plan, do you really want to have to rely on them as your sole source of sustenance over the long haul? A well-rounded mix of the options available to you should be the goal of every food-storage plan. That is why it is advantageous to develop ways to supplement your "off the shelf" food storage with foods you can generate yourself. Having the ability to grow at least some of your own food and preserve it for later use vastly expands your options for having familiar, nutritious and great-tasting food year round. Having a vegetable garden is just one of the methods we use to extend and enhance our emergency food supply, and we will take a closer look at home gardening a bit later, but there are other options worthy of consideration as well.

"The first supermarket appeared on the American landscape in 1946. Until then, where was all the food? ... It was in homes, gardens, local fields, and forests. It was in the pantry, the cellar, the backyard." – Joel Salatin

In addition to having your own vegetable garden, another way to generate some of your own food is by hunting and fishing. As a general statement we, as a society, are mostly detached from where our food actually comes from. I'm certain there are people out there who think the meat that ends up on their plate actually comes from the grocery store in a tidy, pink Styrofoam package because that's the only way they have ever known it to exist. However, in a true disaster situation this facsimile of reality is a luxury that we will no longer be afforded. Much like gardening, hunting is not something you can just decide to go do and expect to have any measure of success. You may not be a hunter today, but if you think the possibility exists that you may have to become one at some point in the future, then hunting is a skill you need to learn now. I did not grow up hunting, and I have not been hunting as an adult, but it is not foreign to me, and I know several people that are hunters. I have come to realize that hunting is a skill that I should add to my toolbox, and I intend to begin my education this fall.

Sometimes the skills that will be of benefit should you ever be faced with a survival situation are also things that we do for fun. Fishing certainly falls into this category. Much like camping teaches us about the importance of having shelter, fishing is a survival skill that we unwittingly practice every time we head to a lake to "drown a few worms." Fishing may not be a skill that will be a good fit for everyone's situation based on the geography of your area, but if you have access to a lake or river, it certainly gives you another option for a source of food, and that makes it a skill worth having.

Other concepts with a more long-range view that would add to your food supply and overall food resilience include creating an edible landscape or adding small stock to your backyard community.

No, I'm not saying you should eat your boxwoods. You can design and build an edible landscape by choosing to grow plants that produce food rather than just pretty flowers. Woody agriculture like fruit and nut trees make a wonderful addition to your living space and are often quite beautiful as well. Instead of planting a Bradford pear tree that's pretty but does not produce fruit, go with a Bartlett pear and set yourself up with great-tasting, fresh pears for years to come. Don't like pears? That's fine. You should grow what you like. The idea remains the same.

Wait, did I suggest that you need to get a cow? No, I did not. However, just because you may not have the space to have a pasture doesn't mean you cannot have a few classic farm animals to help you add depth and richness and even happiness to your food supply. Small stock like chickens, rabbits and goats (just to name a few of your options) are a fantastic way to add a source of food as well as resilience to your long-term plan and nutritious food to your diet right now. Whether you're raising them for meat, eggs or milk, any of the options listed above provide a wonderful and regenerative source of protein. Of course, there are things you would need to learn about the care (and potential processing) of any animal you might choose to keep, but these are certainly viable options should you choose to add them to your plan.

If you really want to extend the food options available to you, I would suggest you take a look at primitive earth skills like trapping and foraging for wild edibles native to your area. Each of these options requires education and training, but you would be hard-pressed to find a more interesting and rewarding motivation to spend a little time wandering through the woods.

To our way of thinking, there is no downside to building and maintaining a supply of stored food in case of an emergency. Of course, you will have food on hand should there be a disaster, but given that food costs are seemingly always on the rise, having a supply of emergency food also serves as a hedge against rising food costs. Since you should be storing the types of food that you're already eating, you can rotate your stored food into your weekly meal plans. This will eliminate the worry of expiration, and "going shopping" will come to take on a whole new meaning around your house. Finally, if your stored food does come up against its expiration date, you can always donate it to a food bank and earn yourself a nice tax write-off. Building and maintaining a supply of stored food is a winning proposition any way you look at it, so why not get started on building yours today?

If you haven't gotten your fill of *"Food Talk with Mr. Powers"* yet, fear not. We'll expand on infrastructure and our philosophies of yum a bit later when we take a look at homesteading. Oh, yes. I'm talking to you. Homesteading.

Chapter 9: COMMUNICATIONS

Campbell placed the ham radio headphones on the communications desk and stood up, his back crackling as he extended fully upright. The past two days hadn't been kind to his aging frame. There was no doubt about that. He'd slept on a cot next to the radios, his Kenwood transceiver scanning preset AM frequencies used by militia groups regionally and nationwide.

Sleep didn't come easy, as reports of civil disorder, fires, and a near complete breakdown of the nation's essential services infrastructure travelled in high frequency radio waves to anyone who cared to listen. Information was spotty at best, but he'd gleaned invaluable information about the event from the airwaves. Cities beyond the Sierra Nevada Mountains in California and the Cascades in the Pacific Northwest seemed to have suffered less of an EMP disruption than the rest of the nation. None of the cities on the West Coast had power, which made sense given the interconnectivity of the nation's electrical grid, but vehicle and home electronics remained mostly unaffected. California was a long way from New England, but it gave Campbell a glimmer of hope. Not all of the country was down for the count.

—From *Event Horizon*

Randall

I'm sure you've been there. I've certainly been there. Something has happened…a car accident, a severe storm, or maybe something worse…and you are separated from a friend or loved one that you fear may have been involved. You quickly try to call just to make sure they're okay, but you can't get through. In an instant, your pulse quickens and the floor begins to tilt as a "just in case" phone call becomes the most important call you can ever remember making. Sometimes the call rings through on the very next try, and all is well. But then, there are those other times when it does not...again and again. It is in those instances that time seems to stand still and the only thing you are aware of is that high-pitched ringing in your ears. Good news or bad news, it doesn't matter at this point. You just want to get through! Not knowing is just the worst. As Pat Frank so eloquently penned in his timeless classic *Alas, Babylon* when Admiral Sam Hazzard is speaking to Helen Bragg about the possible fate of her husband Colonel Mark Bragg, "We inhabit the same purgatory, Mrs. Bragg. The dark level of not knowing."

On March 14th, 2008, a killer tornado tore through downtown Atlanta, Georgia. Among the many events taking place that weekend in Atlanta was the Southeastern Conference basketball tournament, and I was working downtown that night. I was inside when I received a phone call from my wife, Alice, telling me that the local news had broken into programming and radar was showing there was a tornado in downtown Atlanta right now, right on top of me! Being inside a large building, I had no idea anything was going on, and because I'm a bit of a weather fanatic, I had to go see for myself. Alice knew this about me and knew she couldn't keep me from checking things out, but she was going to stay on the line. As I headed outside, I was walking up a set of steps that led to an elevated breezeway that would take me out to the parking lot. There was a revolving door that led to the breezeway and, not knowing what I was going to see through the wall of glass, I was proceeding with caution. By the way, Alice is still on the line with me. Five seconds later, the wings of the revolving door collapsed and smacked together as I was slammed by a wall of wind. I threw my arm up and spun away from the door, expecting to be showered by splinters of glass, but instead I was pelted by dirt, pieces of insulation and other building materials that had been turned into dangerous projectiles by the furious winds of the storm. I stepped to the side and out of the wind-tunnel effect that had been created by the now gaping revolving door. I was still on the call with Alice, and I was trying to describe what was happening all around me when I heard a scream…and it was getting closer. I peeked around the corner and saw a thinly framed security guard being blown down the breezeway, flailing wildly as he was pushed towards the building. Even over the roar of the tornado that was right outside the building, Alice could hear the man's screams too. As the man got closer to the building, his cries were getting louder. Using the increasing sound of the man yelling as a timing mechanism, I reached into the wind tunnel and grabbed the guard to pull him to safety. Alice heard it all. At this point, with the tornado roaring, the man screaming and me being covered with debris, I shouted over the din of the storm to tell Alice, "I'm gonna have to call you back!" Just a few moments later, the tornado passed, and we began to take stock of everyone and assess the damage that was all around us. Very shortly, there were images all over the news showing the destruction that had been wrought in a major American city by a tornado rated as an EF-2 on the Enhanced Fujita scale, packing winds of up to 130 miles per hour. I knew I was safe, but Alice didn't know that. She may have had an idea, but she didn't know. I immediately tried to call her back to let her know I was all right, but my cell phone had no signal. I walked back inside to a landline and tried again. Nothing. Finally, about forty minutes later, I was able to get through to Alice and let her know I was okay. She was glad to hear the good news but quickly let me know that not being able to reach me, especially when you consider the way our call had ended, had not been the best part of her evening. *Point taken.*

That was not the first time I've found myself in an emergency situation, and I am certain it won't be the last. There were several lessons in preparedness learned by everyone in the path of the storm that night, but let's focus on communications after a disaster.

Hey, Steve, back me up on this one, will you? The first step in any traditional military conflict is to take out command and control communications. If you find yourself in the middle of a major disaster situation, you are in a battle for your survival. You are under attack from an event beyond your control as well as the chaos surrounding it. Every military mind on the planet understands the importance of communications in combat. Because of this, they take steps to protect their ability to move information, and they defend against being left deaf and blind with both aggressive and passive measures. A key part of this plan to maintain the ability to communicate is resilience. There are layers and layers of redundancy built into every level of our military operations. As civilians, we may not be able to prevent our interpersonal communications from being disrupted, but we can certainly take steps to build resilience into our lives.

Let's take the easiest option first, telephones. The first option is simple. If you have access to a telephone landline and it is still in working order, use it and reach out to any friends and loved ones to let them know how you're doing. In today's technological age, virtually everyone carries a cell phone on them at all times, and a majority of those phones are smartphones, which means they have more computing capability and connectivity than basic feature phones. Smartphones often feature options like a digital camera, web browsing and the ability to run third-party applications. If you have a smartphone, you should consider downloading emergency alert applications that you can set up to warn you about everything from severe weather to emergency service (police and fire) alerts in your local area. In an emergency situation, every moment counts. In the moments just before and immediately after a disaster, making a call on your cell should be the first method of communication you attempt. If you have a smartphone, you can also use social media apps like Twitter and Facebook to reach out to others to let them know what's going on where you are and whether you're okay. Paired with a smartphone's ability to shoot video and take quality digital pictures, social media like Twitter, Facebook and others also serve as a reporting tool in the immediate aftermath of a disaster. You can document the event on your phone, then upload the videos and pictures to the web for the world to see. This can be helpful in many ways, including helping law enforcement and researchers to better understand what happened during the chaos of the event once things calm down.

Finally, regardless of what type of mobile phone you have, you can still send text messages. Following a disaster, if calls are not going through due to a spike in the volume of calls being attempted or if the cell towers in your area have been disabled or destroyed, you may still have the ability to send and receive text messages. Text messages use less bandwidth on the system than phone calls, and this gives them a better chance of going through. Knowing this, you may want to make texting your first option.

Once the event has ended and using a traditional landline or a cell phone is not an option due to infrastructure failure, you still have options, but they take a bit more planning. Regardless of whether we are talking about a home disaster kit or any version of a mobile survival kit, it should contain a radio that does not require electricity to operate that can be used to receive information. Whether it is battery powered, solar powered or a hand crank model, everyone should have a radio with the ability to receive weather alerts and an emergency broadcast system message. This will help you have a better idea of what's going on in your area beyond what you can see, and information like that is priceless. If you have a battery-powered model, make sure you have fresh batteries in the radio and spare batteries on hand.

Another option for comms post-disaster is two-way radios (Walk 'n' Talks). These can be as simple or complex as you want them to be. You can get models that receive weather alerts, are waterproof or are hands-free. You can decide what works best for you and what best fits your budget. As long as they give you the ability to reach out and talk to someone, and you can count on them when you need them, the model you choose is really inconsequential. Just keep in mind that quality counts, and never more so than after a disaster.

If you're looking for a communications option that's a bit more robust, you should consider Amateur Radio (ham) or Citizens Band (CB) radio. These two options give you a much greater range, and you can get either system in a mobile or stationary rig. If you choose to broadcast as a ham operator, you will need to get an operator's license. However, if you only wish to listen to your shortwave receiver, no license is required. CB radio does not require a license for use. Remember that both systems require electric power to operate after any disaster. Mobile systems can be powered by batteries or your vehicle, but if you have a stationary setup, be sure to include a way to power your rig in your planning.

A tried-and-true method of communication that is often overlooked in the world of preparedness and that is about as analog as they come is handwritten messages. Regardless of the type of disaster you may be facing, pen and paper will still work. Furthermore, keeping a notepad in all of your kits at all times is recommended. You never know when you may have to take down important info, draw a crude map or simply leave a message for someone. We do suggest opting for a waterproof notepad like those offered by *Rite in the Rain* whenever possible, but anything will do in a pinch.

If you really want to take things to a different level when it comes to communications within your family or group, you can develop a cipher or coded messaging system that only the members of your team will understand. On the fun side of things, this is an activity that can be very entertaining and educational for everyone involved. Besides, who wants the *insert name of the big bad invaders here* to know what's going on if we someday find ourselves in the middle of our very own *Red Dawn* world?

An important consideration for anyone that spends a lot of time in the wilderness or thinks that they may someday find themselves lost out there where there are no roads is the concept of directional messaging. In other words, if you get stranded or lost in the woods and you decide to keep moving, you need to remember to leave an obvious indication of which way you are headed by crafting a directional arrow or some other symbol using whatever you have on hand. You can use rocks, limbs, debris, parts from a disabled vehicle or even leave a note (See what I mean?) on a vehicle you leave behind. It doesn't really matter, but the bigger, more colorful and out of place your message appears, the better. This will make it more obvious and give search teams a good idea of where to look for you in their search planning. When you're in a wilderness survival situation, the primary goal is to affect self-rescue and walk out, or get rescued. To that end, you will want to do everything in your power to make sure that happens as quickly as possible, and directional messaging is a skill you need in your back pocket that can help you do just that.

Finally, speaking of low-tech ways to communicate, what about talking to your neighbors? In today's world, we are a society closed off from one another, and that is mostly by choice. We're persuaded to stay shut in our homes by television, video games or the internet, and we really don't have any idea who's living right next door. We want to encourage you to unplug from the matrix for a while and start to build a relationship with the folks you see every day in your community. On a practical level, this information will help you to recon your local area and get a better understanding of where everyone stands in their preparedness and an idea of what resources might be available to you at some point in the future. On a human level, you will find that it is your neighbors and the members of your local community that are the very folks you will be working with following any sort of future disaster. We say build those relationships now because you may be forced to rely on them in the future!

Steven

My cell phone sounds terrible, and I live in the middle of suburbia. Apparently, serving a few thousand people with cellphone coverage in 2014 isn't a priority for the town—or the cell phone carriers that wheel and deal with our elected councilors to win the coverage race. I don't have a lot of confidence that the tower providing me with such "awesome" service will be at the top of anyone's priority list in the event of a disaster.

What about my "landline"? Strike two. I have one of those all-in-one packages through my cable provider. Don't laugh at this obvious flaw in my communications plan. It was the only way I could get all of the channels my kids will NEVER watch for a reasonable price. If the power fails or my router goes down, the phones are useless, which isn't too far from their normal operational status—two of the five phones that came with the base unit are barely charged at any given moment. I wish I could blame lazy kids.

You know what? I like it when the phones don't work or the power goes out. Finally, a little break from email, the latest shows we "have" to watch or the constant nagging of several projects on my computer. Maybe I'm secretly looking forward to an EMP.

Back to the way life should be. Quiet days—just my Kindle and me—and no way to download more books. Damn, I knew there was a downside to e-books (you should order this book in hardcopy). There's a little truth to this paragraph, right? Not the part about wishing for an EMP, but the rest of it. When the power goes out for a few hours, it's kind of relaxing. Just you and your family, until right around the three-hour mark. Then the questions start flying. What's going on? When is the power coming back? Why did the power go out? Is there a crispy squirrel somewhere or did "the terrorists" finally shoot out enough power station transformers to crash the grid?

Nobody likes being out of the loop for too long. I start looking for answers right away. Fortunately, cell phones continue to function during the typical power outage scenario, allowing you to talk with a friend on the other side of town and confirm that the world as we know it remains intact. What if you couldn't use your cell phone? *The world gets a little smaller when your communication range is reduced to walking across the street and knocking on your neighbor's door.*

In the event of a disaster causing an extended loss of power, communicating beyond shouting distance will be a problem. For many reasons, that's the worst time to lose a capability we take for granted. What if this happens during the middle of the day, when the kids are in school and you're at work? The scenarios are endless, and frankly, there's not much you can do about it. The options for portable, emergency two-way long-distance communications are expensive—essentially limited to satellite phones.

Before you throw in the towel or break out the credit card, remember the key mantra of this book. SURVIVE WHAT? A scenario knocking out cell phone coverage is highly unlikely. The cellular system might experience overload with everyone calling at once, but you can usually sneak a text through the data stream—***important to remember***. Since not every family is going to buy four satellite phones and the voice plans to go with them ($400 for a refurbished phone and $25 monthly emergency plan), we're going to assume that you will read chapter fifteen and put together an effective disaster plan that gets everyone home or to a designated rally point. Now what?

Most of us will be limited to one-way long-range communications. A portable emergency/weather radio is a good option. Every family should have one, preferably the kind that you can hand-crank to charge. This is the most basic option, which will give you access to emergency broadcasts. A handheld scanner is another layer, allowing you in some cases to listen to local emergency responders. A good scanner will come with preset frequencies in several useful frequency bands. Police, fire/emergency, ham, marine, railroad, Civil Air, Military Air and CB radio (10-4 good buddy!). You might get lucky and stumble across a few sources transmitting some highly useful information.

What if you want to talk to them? Now it gets a little more complicated. For the frequency bands listed above, you're mostly out of luck with the exception of marine, Civil Air, ham and CB radio frequencies. The problem here is that you'll need a separate radio for each. Please prove me wrong on this. I don't think you can, unless you "illegally" modify a ham radio to transmit on CB, Civil Air and marine frequencies. As much as I'd like to talk to the outside world when a disaster strikes, my more immediate need for communication lies at home, so I'll focus there—for now.

Once I get my family in one place, I'd like to keep them there. Obviously, I can't tie us all together like "one of those families" we've all seen at the airport. Bathroom time will be a little awkward. The next best solution is a family-sized set of inexpensive "walkie-talkies," also known as two-way radios. Perfect for the house, neighborhood and slightly beyond (some are advertised to reach sixteen miles—good luck with that). We use these while camping and boating, for the rare occasion when our interests diverge. Alex Fletcher often incorporated two-way radios for the same purpose, in addition to tactical communications with his two buddies, Ed and Charlie.

Is anyone mad at me for not giving ham radio its due respect earlier in the chapter? You didn't spend the time and money on an amateur radio certification for nothing, right? There's a reason I pushed it down the list. Everything I've mentioned so far is portable. I'm big on portability, especially when it comes to the technology-driven topic of communications. With a good scanner, satellite phone, and a few two-way radios, you can carry your communications needs in a fanny pack (or whatever they're called). Don't jump on me about the handheld ham radios. I'll get there. I want to address the base station type of ham radio that can put you in touch with Siberia, because that's the only type most of us consider when we hear the words "ham radio."

I hear you yelling at me. "He's prejudiced against ham radio because he can't fit it in his pocket. I'm talking to China! Good luck doing that when your beloved system of satellites have fallen from the sky!" I hear you. Ham gives the operator access to thousands of ham users around the world (if you know what you're doing), without reliance on anything but radio waves. Not a bad deal at all, but let's be honest. Are you going to do this? It's not overly expensive, but you do need a license, which requires a test. I barely get my car registered on time every year—I often rely on a lenient police officer to "remind" me.

Ham also requires practice and skill to effectively talk with anyone outside of town. Most prepper websites stress this aspect of ham radio, and I concur. I spent two years in a specialized U.S. Marine Corps unit that lived and died by communications. HF, VHF and UHF with dozens of antennae configurations and power amplification setups. There's a reason the marines have a specialized career path in communications. Longer distance communication using radio waves is an art. I view ham radio as one of the last pieces of your personal preparedness plan, but a sweet one if you have it in place or are willing to take the steps to effectively employ one. I don't want to completely talk you out of ham radio, but I do want to put it in perspective compared to your other communications needs. SURVIVE WHAT?

Handheld ham radios might be a more realistic option if you like the idea of amateur radio. Since they have a limited transmit range (five to ten miles under the best conditions), they function more like a two-way radio, and you won't have your hopes dashed when you can't talk to Brisbane, Australia. Hopefully, you can contact a friendly and competent ham operator within your transmit range, who will share regional, national and possibly international information.

Of course, all of these handy-dandy items require electricity for continued operations, which brings us to the next essay.

Chapter 10: ENERGY

"We have Emily and Ethan watching the connection in the barn. You never know...Alex's log indicates that the bank of panels on the barn have never been tested with this gear. They have a fire extinguisher," said Samantha.

"Mom, it's fine. The electricity is already flowing from the panels through the barn. This won't change anything," said Abby, shaking her head. "Ready?"

"Go for it," said Kate.

Abby flipped the transfer switch, and nothing happened at the circuit breaker box. She pointed behind them at two side-by-side LED monitors wired to the battery bank, which consisted of 16 deep-cell, 12-Volt AGM batteries mounted on a thick wooden table in the center of the room. Red and black wires ran back and forth across the batteries, in a pattern that made little sense to Kate. She believed they were connected in parallel, whatever that meant. The monitors showed green numbers, which she assumed was a good sign.

"It's charging. The one on the left is set to measure the charging current and the one on the right is a multifunction monitor. It's showing 12.6 volts, which means the battery bank is about ninety percent charged. Based on the calculations in Mr. Fletcher's book, the system is rated to provide 2880 amp hours, which should be enough to run lights at night, the security equipment, the pump for the well, and other appliances if absolutely necessary. Long term, we'll have to closely monitor the charge and discharge rates. It's all in the book. We should probably take a close look," said Abby.

Everyone clapped and congratulated Abby, who looked slightly embarrassed, but continued.

"We replaced the controller, inverter and both monitors, but we don't have any more backups."

"Is the system still vulnerable to an EMP?" said Kate.

"We disconnected the grid-tie inverter, but according to Mr. Fletcher's book, the wires connecting the panels to the house will probably conduct enough of the EMP to fry everything. If we get hit again, we're out of luck."

"Well, I doubt that'll happen. How many times in one lifetime do you get EMP'd?" said Tim.

—From *Event Horizon*

Steven

We have a little game in our house called "swap the batteries." Any device powered by AA or AAA batteries is included in this "game." The rules are simple.

1. Everyone plays.

2. When the batteries in a device are dead, you replace them with the batteries in the nearest functional device.

3. The TV remotes are off-limits until the very end.

4. Have fun! (That's always a rule in our house.)

When I pick up the TV remote and it feels light, I don't bother to press the button or check the other remotes. I know for a fact that every battery in the house has been diverted to my son's Xbox controllers or my daughter's pink walkie-talkies.

There's a hidden silver lining to all of this. Unwritten Rule 5. ***The kids never cannibalize the flashlight batteries.*** I joke about the remotes (if swearing is considered joking), but I've never warned them about the flashlights. They understand the value of light in a power outage, because they've experienced the sensation firsthand. We lose power three or four times a year. At least one of those outages lasts five to twelve hours. Hardly a "disaster," but when the big light bulb in the sky goes away at the end of the day, you have to carry a flashlight around the house.

On a scale of one to ten, losing the ability to flood the inside of your house with unflattering fluorescent light bulbs scores a big fat ONE as a disaster. Didn't people live like this for millennia before the widespread distribution of electricity?

Of course. Life was a lot less complicated back in the Civil War era. Not easier. Less complicated. Homes were heated by wood or coal-burning stoves, and oil lamps or candles provided most of the lighting. That was the entire sum of a home's ENERGY needs. Things are a little different today. In the event of a power loss later tonight, we have furnaces to run, refrigerators to keep cold, and a whole host of electronic devices to operate. I take a three-tier approach to this "problem." What a surprise. The RULE OF THREES again.

Important note that applies to the rest of this essay. If the weather is fine, and you've ruled out "societal breakdown" as the cause of the power failure, you can get in your car and drive until you find an area with power. Frankly, most of you will still be driving to work at this point. "My house doesn't have power" doesn't hold a lot of weight with project deadlines looming at the cubicle farm. Please keep this in mind, because much of what I'm going to say may feel like I subscribe to the "bunker" mentality. I don't. My brother-in-law lives in Vermont. Can you say, "Unexpected house guests?"

The first tier handles a temporary loss of power (twelve hours to two days) due to a thunderstorm, windstorm or a blizzard—the vast majority of power-loss scenarios. I have a saying (which I didn't invent) that goes something like this. "I can stand on my head for two days if I have to." I can't stand on my head for more than twenty minutes, but I use this phrase when the kids complain about going without TV for a day or Wi-Fi access for an hour. The point: *You can endure some changes and perceived discomfort for a reasonable period of time.*

Even in the dead of winter, you can bundle up or burrow under blankets. No fireplace or wood-burning stove required (though highly recommended). Don't believe me? Neither does my wife. Ever go on vacation and turn your heat down to 50 degrees? Whenever we return from a winter vacation, the house is at 54 degrees, even in the middle of February. That's a livable temperature with a few layers of warm clothing, though I will admit, it feels like subarctic temperatures when it's inside your home.

What else? The water still runs, and you can cook food. Our stove runs on propane, but anyone can crack out a camping stove (ventilate the area, please) and heat up a can of SpaghettiOs for the family. You might feel like the Road Warrior in an apocalyptic wasteland, but it's really not a big deal. You're basically camping in your house, without the hundred-foot hike to the campground's messy bathroom.

Battery-powered flashlights and camping lamps combined with a few strategically placed candles can get you from point A to point B in your house just fine. For entertainment, you can pull out the hand-cranked emergency radio or scanner and listen for updates. Additionally, you probably have cell coverage at this point. Use your phone judiciously to talk with friends about the situation, check websites and communicate via social media. Remember, you can charge cell phones using your car. Just keep the garage bay open and the door to the house closed if you need to turn your car on to charge devices.

Here's the controversial part. You don't need to run a generator yet (even if you have one), unless you have to run a sump pump during a rainstorm. I have friends with powerful whole-house generators that start the instant the power stops. The lights don't flicker and the central air keeps pumping gloriously dehumidified, cold air into their house. Sounds nice—if you can afford the price tag ($5–10K). There are much less expensive, portable generator setups.

Tier-two power considerations kick in after day two. This is the start of my SURVIVE WHAT scenario. If they can't restore power within forty-eight hours, you could start to face bigger problems. In cold temperatures, your pipes could freeze and burst, which could put a serious dent in your comfortable camping experience. Charging radios, scanners and cell phones may present a challenge, as these items are used more frequently to determine the big picture outside of your house. Your comfort level and morale will decrease significantly. Is any of this truly life threatening? Not if you have the rest of THE BASICS covered (food, water, first aid, shelter), which is my primary goal.

For prolonged power outages (out to ten days or so), I focus on morale once the BASICS are addressed. A battery bank can power your furnace for an extended period of time, providing hot water for showers. Everybody appreciates a hot shower. We can run the fan on our propane fireplace with the batteries, which heats the entire first floor with a minimal charge expenditure compared to running the furnace. It's more than enough to keep the pipes from freezing and the kids from complaining. We can also charge all of the personal electronics, which keeps everyone occupied to some degree. The battery bank can be connected to the grid (charge maintained when the power was flowing) or solar panels (continuous charging in the absence of grid power).

I say batteries, you say generator. I'm cool with that. Either choice accomplishes the same goal for my SURVIVE WHAT scenario. And to show that I'm not biased, I'll say this—*the generator gives you way more power for a longer period of time, for the same price or less.* You have to keep it running with gasoline from containers unless you can hook it up to natural gas or propane (great options), but that's not a big deal for a well-maintained generator. I say batteries because it fits in with my long-term, **tier-three** preparedness plan.

Tier three is where we get serious and discuss two considerations. Long-term power needs (electrical infrastructure wrecked by natural disaster or taken out by solar flare/EMP/snipers) and portable power needs if you decide to bug out. This is Alex Fletcher-level preparedness. I'm going to level with everyone. This is where I split with the Fletchers. I don't have a philosophical disagreement with my alter ego; I have slightly different priorities.

Alex Fletcher invested money in a solar power system in *The Jakarta Pandemic* to protect his family from a possible pandemic. In real life, Steven Konkoly bought a sailboat to spend guaranteed time with his family on Casco Bay during the summer. I'm not saying he's wrong and I'm right. We're both one and the same, sort of. If the power went out tomorrow and stayed out for the rest of the year, I'd have to say that Alex was right and I didn't listen—or I was right, but I didn't listen to myself.

Alex's ENERGY plan in *The Jakarta Pandemic* and *The Perseid Collapse* series represents the pinnacle of what I imagine a family might require in the absence of grid-generated electricity. You can always go bigger and better, but a rooftop solar panel array connected to a sizable battery bank gives you a wide array of options to address "indefinite," basic power needs.

What about portable energy needs? I include this in tier three, because it signifies a major event requiring you to leave your house—this doesn't include a temporary relocation to a hotel nine miles away for comfort reasons. We're talking about an event that ***forces*** you to evacuate your house. Civil disorder, major natural disaster destroying your home or rendering your area unsafe—use your imagination. I'll keep this part simple. *You want the ability to power flashlights and communications gear.* All of this equipment is powered by replaceable batteries or internally charged batteries. You need a way to handle both. Here comes a RULE OF THREES within my three-tier system. Bonus.

1. I recommend a decent supply of disposable batteries to power your flashlights. Quick and easy.

2. Beyond that, you should consider investing in rechargeable batteries. If you're on the road or in temporary shelter for an extended period of time, you'll run out of disposable batteries at some point. Some of you are raising your eyebrows. How do I charge the batteries?

3. With a portable solar-panel charging station. This is not a fixed panel attached to a neck brace and worn over your head. The technology is amazing, and some very potent (small-device oriented) solar-charging systems are no bigger than the hardcopy version of this book. You can also use these systems to charge all of your other communications devices.

Are you tired of reading about power? I'm tired of talking about it. I think I've covered the basics, but I'll turn you over to Randy, because he generally knows far more than I do.

Randall

What is energy? Practically speaking, energy is defined as the capacity to do work. So, if you're going to get about the work of surviving any disruption, emergency or disaster situation, you're going to have to have energy. Nothing happens without it.

Energy is a key component of any preparedness plan. Whether we're talking about the big-ticket items like keeping the lights on in your house or having the fuel on hand to power vehicles and tools, to the smaller (but just as important) things like having the batteries or fuel necessary to keep your flashlights and radios operational, you've got to have energy.

From fire to food to liquid fuels, energy comes in many forms. How you choose to power your preparedness plan is up to you, and the preparedness prism will serve as your guide. Once your plans are in place, choose the method of power generation that is the best fit and then learn how to use it.

If you're planning to stay in your home and ride out the disaster, you will be in good shape as long as the electrical grid is functioning, but you will need a plan in case you were to lose power. If you're looking for a long-term answer to any future power disruptions, adding an array of solar panels to your preparedness infrastructure may be the option for you. If the cost of the solar option is a prohibitive one for you, another reliable source of backup power is a generator. There are solar generator models available that use photovoltaic panels to charge a battery that can be used as a source of power, or there are the more traditional generators that run on liquid fuels, just be sure to store the appropriate amounts of fuel necessary to run the generator if you choose a traditional option.

If you are forced to leave your home or if your plan calls for a mobile option, you are still going to need a way to power and charge your gear. Radios, headlamps, cell phones, laptops, tablets, handheld GPS devices…all devices that could find their way into your BOLT kit…and each of them need a power source or need to have the ability to create their own power. In addition to making sure you have batteries in the right sizes and quantities to power your equipment, you may want to consider gear that can generate its own power, such as a hand-crank radio or flashlight. Another option for power on the go is a portable solar power pack kit like those made by Goal ZERO. These powerful, lightweight solar systems are a fantastic addition to any mobile disaster kit.

When it comes to energy needs in most disaster situations, the ability to start a fire, having a quality flashlight and a small radio with new batteries, plus a few cans of fuel for a camping stove will be enough to get you through the event. Your level of preparedness only improves if you've got a generator (and plenty of fuel if necessary) on hand, and you can easily scale your preparations up to any level from there. Whatever your energy needs when it comes to preparedness, remember the power is within your reach.

Chapter 11: SELF-DEFENSE

"He can't keep the Raven up in this weather. Five pounds is no match for heavy rain and gusting winds. He'd rather recover it in Cambridge than retrieve it from the river or a hostile street. Frankly, I'm surprised it's still flying. I'm going to strip down my tactical rig and stuff it in my backpack so I look a little friendlier on the streets. The two of you should be fine."

Ryan wore a gray T-shirt under a light blue, unbuttoned long-sleeve hiking shirt, a pair of khaki pants with cargo pockets and brown leather boots. With a medium-sized military-style rucksack and Alex's desert MARPAT boonie hat, he might attract a second look, which was why Alex insisted that he stuff the HK P30, without suppressor, into his right cargo pocket. Tucking it into his front waistband was too obvious, and the rear waistband was obstructed by his pack. It was all about appearances and practicality, which brought him to Chloe.

Her backpack was a purple, off the shelf, day hiking rig, which didn't raise an eyebrow. Combined with a light blue Boston Red Sox hat, gray short-sleeved hiking shirt and dark brown convertible cargo pants, she looked like a lost, yuppie hiker. Her outfit wasn't the problem. Chloe's gender would automatically attract attention, and additional scrutiny could end in disaster. Wrong. Any scrutiny could be instantly lethal.

—From *Event Horizon*

Randall

No matter where you live, your home is your castle. I am certain that each and every one of us would do whatever we had to do to protect our homes. If there are friends or loved ones we must protect, this urge will be even stronger. However, we can't be at home all of the time, and we can't always be there to protect our loved ones. What if a threat presents itself and you're not at home? What if you're on vacation, at work, or just at your local supermarket parking lot? What if you suffer a home invasion and no one is at home? Do you have security measures in place that will deter criminals from making your home their primary target? There are countless scenarios that you must consider when it comes to self-defense and security.

The ability to defend oneself is an undeniable individual right. How you go about doing it is up to you. There are a wide range of options in this area from taking personal defense classes to firearms to other less lethal force methods. Planning for self-defense is a very personal decision that should not be taken lightly. It is our goal to help you fully understand your options as you work through your decision-making process. Once again, we turn to the Practical Tactical Preparedness Prism to help us along. By sorting out the planning, purpose of use (POU), and practice involved with the self-defense options available, you will more easily be able to identify the best choice for you.

Let's apply the KISS method to start and keep the concept of self-defense simple. For our purposes in this discussion, think of self-defense and self-preservation as interchangeable terms with the top priority always being keeping yourself and your friends and family safe from harm. Whenever possible, the very best option for self-defense is to avoid any possible threat altogether. This goes hand in hand with the concept of situational awareness. By staying aware of what's going on around you at all times, you will give yourself the opportunity to recognize the possible threat at a distance and simply remove yourself from the potentially dangerous situation before you are ever in danger. Whether you are at home or out in public, every member of your family or group can do their part by staying aware and alert at all times. The more eyes and ears you have gathering information, the better, because you never know who might see or hear something that will make the difference between being in a dangerous situation and having a wonderfully event-free day. If the situation dictates this is not possible and you find yourself facing an immediate threat of harm, I would still say that the primary goal would be to escape the situation and get away from the threat. I know I don't want to get into extended hand-to-hand combat with a foe I know nothing about. What would be the point? Would it be to prove that I'm tougher than my attacker? That risk/reward assessment doesn't seem worth it to me. My goal would be to get separation, get away and get help if necessary. Self-preservation and safety, those are the priorities.

However, if we're being honest with ourselves, we must admit that we could someday find ourselves in a dangerous situation that simply does not allow for conflict evasion or escape. There is an imminent threat, and we are only left with one option. We must fight.

After acknowledging this hard fact of reality, the next step is to settle on the method of self-defense that you are most comfortable with. You may not like violence. Well, here's a news flash...most of us don't. But I have to ask the question, what wouldn't you do to protect your friends and loved ones from someone attempting to do them harm or take the resources necessary for their survival? This is the big one, and you have to be honest with yourself to discover the real answer. Once you figure out the answer to this question, the rest of this self-defense discussion will fall into place.

When you think about self-defense, you have to consider all that means. For most people that process has two parts, home defense and personal defense. There are several options for home defense, including everything from a baseball bat or bear spray to a firearm such as a shotgun, based on your comfort level. It does not matter which method you choose to protect your home, but we do believe you need some way to defend your castle. I will say this. If you believe that it is a good idea to have the ability to defend your home, when looking at the options I mentioned above as an example, my question is why would you ever allow the threat to get close enough to you or your loved ones to use the baseball bat? If given the option, I know I would not make that choice.

When it comes to personal defense, we recommend knowing a few basic hand-to-hand self-defense techniques regardless of your gender or size. Regardless of the level of damage your chosen method of personal defense could produce, knowing what to do to escape an attacker and having the confidence to do it could prove the difference between life and death before you ever even have the chance to deploy your primary personal defense method.

If you choose to arm yourself with a personal defense weapon, I would caution you to remember that the key phrase we are discussing here is *self-defense*. For most of us, it is not our job to make the streets safer for the general public or take the law into our own hands. Regardless of what tool you choose as your self-defense weapon, the top priority is still to keep yourself, your family and friends safe from harm and nothing more.

It honestly does not matter whether you choose to carry pepper spray, a baton or a handgun for personal defense. That decision is yours and yours alone and should be based on your personal comfort level and the situations you may be planning for. What does matter for everyone is that you get the training necessary to safely and effectively deploy your personal defense tool. **It is your responsibility!** For instance, if you choose to carry a firearm and do not get the training necessary to ensure that you can carry it and (if necessary) put it into action safely, then I would argue you are as much a danger to your fellow innocent citizens as the bad guy. Don't be that person. Furthermore, you should practice with your chosen method of personal defense so that you will know you can count on your tool and your skills should you ever be forced to rely on them. This concept is pretty simple. When faced with a stressful situation and forced to act under duress, you will default to your level of training. If you are going to trust your life to a personal defense technique or tool, you should have no doubt about your skill or its capabilities should you ever be forced to use it.

Home security is another aspect of self-defense that should be considered, and it is different than home defense. If you are forced to resort to a home-defense option, then your home security has already been compromised. No home is impenetrable, and every home can be broken into. When it comes to home security, there are layers. The first step is to do all you can to make your home look like a tough nut to crack, or at least like a less appealing target than the next house on the street. That's a harsh way to look at it, but it is reality. Criminals will most often take the easiest prize available to them, and anything you can do to harden your home's defenses is a positive step towards securing your castle. A home security system won't stop a home invader from breaking in, but it may deter them from trying. Having a loud and barking dog or two could also be enough to make a criminal move along in search of an easier target. Covering the basics like locking your doors and windows, adding multiple dead bolts to your doors at different height levels, reinforcing door frames and adding motion-activated lights around your property are all inexpensive steps you can take today that will greatly improve the security of your home and the areas surrounding it.

Self-defense is a broad, but very important topic, and there is never simply one life at risk. With variables like personal choice dictating your approach, budget limitations and the age and physical limitations of your family or group to consider, it is also one of the most difficult to get a good handle on, but all hope is not lost. Using the preparedness prism as a guide and working through the process of the Practical Tactical Preparedness Cycle one step at a time, you can find the best self-defense option for your situation and scale it to fit all of your needs. At home or away, with your group or alone, you will be able to rest easy knowing you have done all you can to keep the most important people in your life safe. Remember, the top priority should always be keeping yourself and your friends and family safe from harm. That is victory. Develop a plan, be aware of your situation at all times, and commit to the level of training necessary to be proficient in the method of self-defense you have chosen. Don't be a victim, be victorious.

Steven

Finally, we get to talk about guns! Everyone knows this book is a thinly veiled disguise for me to roll out Alex Fletcher's next level of personal defense. Has anyone seen the movie *Predator*? That's right; book seven in *The Perseid Collapse Series* will feature "Old Painless." If you don't know what that is, Google "predator old painless" and have a laugh. Are you chuckling? Get it out, because I'm about to pull the rug out from under you. Civilians can and do own weapons like that. Gulp. Fortunately, they can't be hauled around on foot—too easily. I hope that puts things into perspective.

You will always find someone with a bigger gun and more training. Your time is far better spent focusing on the plan you've created to handle your SURVIVE WHAT scenario. Here we go.

Nearly anyone can buy a military-style rifle, tactical gear and ammunition, even in severely restricted states. Have money—have guns, unless you have a criminal record. Queue up the Yoda voice. "Having a high-speed rifle and lots of ammunition does not a better prepper make." That's Yoda speak for—*the topic of self-defense is far more complicated than arming yourself with a fancy rifle and assuming everything will be fine.* Without the proper training and mindset, it won't be fine. I can almost guarantee it.

Remember Randy's **Kit to Fit** concept? No chapter is better served by Randy's mantra than Self-Defense. Randy's attitude about the role of firearms in the self-defense part of any personal readiness plan is what first drew me toward taking a close look at a collaborative book. Not everyone is a former marine like Alex Fletcher, with the skills to effectively employ a military-style rifle from the start.

Before we talk about firearms and their *possible* role in your preparedness plan, let's look at some other aspects of self-defense. Don't groan. You'll learn something. I can almost guarantee it (the lawyers kept me from making a full guarantee). Specifically, I'd like to explore two strategies that cover opposite sides of the spectrum. At home or on the road, a survival situation can rapidly change in the blink of an eye. It's a fluid environment, requiring flexibility and a honed ability to "test the winds." What works in one situation is unlikely to work in the next. The next few paragraphs will describe "passive" measures you can take to discourage the need to employ the active ones that might require you to reload magazines later.

My favorite tactic is one I learned in the navy. As our ship's unofficial security officer (more of a concerned advocate), I constantly struggled with the security in foreign port—especially when tied alongside a pier in the Middle East. Bottom line, one .45 caliber pistol (unloaded) stood between a highly trained terrorist cell and the entire ship. Scary.

When we spent time in the Arabian Gulf, we were directed to take a more proactive stance. Once again, leadership balked at adding additional weapons, opting to add a few more sailors to roam the topside decks. Marginally effective at best. I argued for sailors with rifles, but the resounding answer was NO. "We don't need the liability of junior sailors carrying loaded weapons around." When I heard that, I immediately said, "Then don't issue ammunition. If you're going to have them walking around where everyone can see them, at least have them carrying something." The next question was "how many is enough?" Easy answer. "One more than the ship next to us. Make us the harder target."

That's the strategy, ladies and gentlemen, if you're facing a likely and unavoidable threat. ***Make it clear that you're not the easy mark.*** At home, post signs, police tape around the yard, make at least one of your "weapons" visible while you're outside—do more than your neighbor or the same if they're already at that level. Your actions could be as simple as standing in the doorway with binoculars and pointing at the perceived threat. **Let them know you care!**

This same strategy can be applied on the road. Normally, you'd do everything in your power to NOT draw attention to yourself, but when it's clear (or you suspect) that you're under extra scrutiny, give them a little something to think about. Start at the low end of the scale with a knowing look and a scowl. Graduate to flashing some hardware if that doesn't work. Potential threats will size you up quickly if they take an interest. You want to take an active role in that decision-making process.

Do you feel a little uncomfortable with this? You should. It's confrontation and should be employed as a next-to-last strategy—before people get hurt. It's not my favorite strategy. Far from it. Contrary to the impression I may have given you, I'm not confrontational. I'd much rather blend in or sneak by than run the risk of an encounter. Let me share the strategy you should strive to employ most of the time. *Avoidance.*

Doesn't sound very apocalyptic, does it? Trust me, you'll be glad you read this paragraph, because surviving a disaster, short or long term, is more about avoiding attention than attracting it. Personally, I don't think Alex Fletcher did a very good job of this in *The Jakarta Pandemic.* He pissed off neighbors and let it slip that he had a sizable stockpile of food and medical supplies. If he'd kept his mouth completely shut at the neighborhood meeting in the book, the story might have turned out differently—probably a lot more boring. Not good for selling books. I thought it would be more interesting for readers to learn from Alex's mistakes. This was by far his worst lapse of judgment, and it nearly got him killed.

Avoidance comes in many forms and requires you to stand back and study your situation. In the earlier stages of a longer term disaster, it might make more sense to keep the generator noise to a minimum by running it during the day or for fixed periods of time. Not everyone will have a generator, and the last thing you want is to keep that cranky neighbor up all night with your generator noise. He's sweating in his sheets, thinking about your air-conditioning and the rest of the goodies you have stashed away. Likewise, a backyard barbeque on day eighteen of a regional power outage might not be the best idea. I guarantee someone is eating his or her last can of beans. You get the picture. "Stay below the radar." Some measures of avoidance are not as obvious as others. Spend some time thinking about this.

On the road, you want to "go grey," which means wearing clothing and carrying gear that doesn't overtly identify you as a "survivor." Grey is neutral. That's how you want to look. "Going grey" can look different based on the circumstances. Alex Fletcher employed this strategy when escorting his son and Ed's daughter out of Boston. He still carried a rifle and a backpack, but he removed the marine-issued tactical vest and pistol holster. Alex hoped to look like a well-prepared father escorting his family to safety. Not an uncommon sight given what happened forty-eight hours earlier.

We talk about 72-hour packs and BOLT kits (a little later) in this book. By necessity, they hold an abundant amount of gear. It's hard to hide something like that, but does your pack have to be the latest issue military equipment? Can you accomplish the same goal with an off-the-shelf commercial version? A few enterprising companies sell military-style, civilian color backpacks. The goal is to fit in with the rest of the people on the road as best as possible without dressing in high-top shoes, sweatpants and a "Who Farted?" T-shirt.

Now for the main event! FIREARMS. Who skipped to this part? I made it easy by putting the words FIREARMS in capital letters. This is where **Kit to Fit** really comes into play. If you're first readiness purchase is a civilian version of the HK416 assault rifle—you're one lucky son of a—sorry, I got carried away for a moment. Let me start again. You have a damn fine rifle in your hands, but you need to learn how to use it to be any more effective than your neighbor's compound bow (that's not a dig against bows). Even if you think you know how to use it, you're probably overestimating your ability. Like any skill, shooting and firearms handling is a perishable skill. You don't want to perish with it. If you start on this end of the self-defense spectrum, resist the temptation to *Fit the Kit*. Learn to use the weapon from the ground up and figure out where it fits into your overall plan, instead of creating a plan around the rifle. *I feel safe saying that most of our initial SURVIVE WHAT plans don't require a firearm, especially a military-style rifle.* As your SURVIVE WHAT scenario changes, you'll be hard-pressed to realistically avoid a firearm.

So what do I recommend? What's the best weapon? Pistol? Shotgun? What kind of training? How does Steven Konkoly roll? I'm going to cheat you slightly at this point. At least I admit it in advance. I won't give specific recommendations, because the solution will be different for everyone. **Kit to Fit** doesn't just apply to your personal preparedness plan, it takes into account the realistic abilities and attitudes of the individual. I recommend that you seek out a well-regarded firearms instructor or a personal readiness consulting team, like Randy Power's Practical Tactical, to figure this out. Randy works with a firearms/tactical instructor to round out this aspect of his service. They work with the client to ensure **Kit to Fit.**

I can't stress this enough. A good instructor will expose you to different types of firearms and determine the best fit. Don't be disappointed if a firearm isn't recommended. Frankly, a firearm is not for everyone. I'm not a certified instructor, but I applied the same approach to helping a firearms-naïve couple decide what type of firearm to bring on a sailing trip through the Northwest Passage (across the Arctic Ocean from the Pacific to Atlantic). They needed to choose between a shotgun or a .308 rifle.

Laws in Canada and Greenland require one of the two for protection against polar bears. I guess you don't have the right to be eaten without a fight up there. Long story short, after firing the shotgun, the wife was leery of the whole proposition, but felt it was manageable. I started with the shotgun on purpose. After one round (fired by me) through the .308, she didn't need to see anymore. The kick and physical blast of the .308 (you can feel the pressure wave for several feet) told her that it wouldn't work—and she didn't have to bruise her shoulder. Easy day for everyone. They settled on a pump-action shotgun similar to the one we used, and scheduled "real" training in Seattle. That's **Kit to Fit** in action.

So, to summarize the entire chapter: Avoid trouble, but carry a stick that you can effectively employ to defend your party. Whatever you carry, keep training in as practical of an environment as possible. Targets don't hang conveniently in front of you in the real shooting world. I've spoken my peace—not really. I have a surprise essay buried in one of the later topics that further explores self-defense. You'll want to read it.

Chapter 12: FIRST AID

Portland's situation seemed no different than that of the rest of the nation. Every treatment facility was overwhelmed, understaffed, and days away from exhausting all critical medical supplies. Federal and state emergency supply packages couldn't meet the demand and would likely be exhausted within the next few weeks. The country was on the brink of a complete breakdown, and New England was now facing a storm system that most meteorologists agreed would be a uniquely devastating early season storm.

—From *The Jakarta Pandemic*

Steven

I'm not a doctor—nor do I play one in my books. You won't find any medical advice in this chapter, but if you come across something perceived to be such, refer back to the first sentence of this essay. You might be shaking your head. No medical advice on how to beat the next super-pandemic or conduct emergency heart-bypass surgery one hundred feet below the ground in my bunker? Sorry, you'll have to research those topics on Yahoo Answers. For now, we'll stick to the very basics. If you're a medical professional, you don't get to skip this chapter. You'll see why very shortly.

Do three Band-Aids and a quarter bottle of pain relievers pretty much summarize the full extent of your home medical kit? With kids in the house, you might be able to add a tube of triple antibiotic ointment to the mix. Am I still in the ballpark? If you purchased one of those expensive, home first-aid kits a few years ago, add a small cold pack, tweezers, a few odd-sized Band-Aids and a pair of sterile gloves to the arsenal. All in all, barely enough to get you through one minor spill on your bicycle. Trust me, you're not alone. For years, this is exactly how the Konkolys rolled. Finding a Band-Aid in our house involved ransacking five drawers, two cabinets, one purse, a backpack and both cars. By the time we found a Band-Aid, Mother Nature had already stopped the bleeding through the miracle of coagulation. This reminds me of a universal truth—***all wounds, big and small, quit bleeding eventually***, though not always because of the body's marvelous ability to repair itself.

I kind of mixed Band-Aids with life-threatening wounds in the last paragraph. Not a good combination. If your takeaway was "we need more Band-Aids in the house," you're on the right track, but the finish line is somewhere over the next hill. As long as one of your SURVIVE WHAT goals isn't to provide cradle-to-grave healthcare coverage for everyone in your bunker, the finish line may not be as far away as you think.

I always start small and work my way up, trying not to duplicate effort. I suggest you take the same approach. Over a period of three months, I pieced together (several small purchases during regular grocery runs) a robust kit that fits in a football-sized military pouch (waterproof) designed to clip onto a backpack or belt. We throw this in the car for trips, or bring it on the sailboat. I can reasonably treat several deep cuts, along with a variety of ailments or incidents with the kit. Snake bites, bee stings, burns, fever, poison ivy/oak, diarrhea, and seasickness—minor stuff. Here's the catch. Nobody touches this kit in the house unless there's an emergency. That's the rule. With one kit intact at all times, I've covered most of our bug out needs and developed the kit I need for my most likely SURVIVE WHAT scenario.

Of course, I take it a few steps further. Next to my bug out stash is an old backpack filled with additional supplies. Motrin, Tylenol, Sudafed, antihistamines, gloves, masks, assorted size and shaped bandages, compresses, triangular bandages, medical tape, scissors, scalpels, antiseptic solution, antibiotic ointment, gauze, eyewash, thermometer, hand sanitizer, several first aid manuals, instant cold packs, and alcohol wipes. Sound familiar? Alex Fletcher had the same items on his shelves. If you can get your hands on some antibiotics or antivirals, all the better.

Kit to Fit still applies here! Do you have a medical condition that requires medication like diabetes or asthma? Don't forget to address these needs in your first aid readiness plan.

A few more words about first aid. If you have access to professional medical care, don't hesitate to seek it. There's a reason doctors and nurses spend years in medical school! First aid is a balancing act, and it's called FIRST aid for a reason. It's the first thing you do! It's not meant to be First, Second and Last Aid if other options exist. Of course, you may not always have a choice. A first aid guide oriented toward outdoor/wilderness survival can serve as a fantastic reference for the treatment of broken bones, severe bleeding and head injuries. Type survival medicine into Amazon or Google and consider adding one of these guides to your collection.

Beyond that, taking a one- to two-day emergency/trauma first response course designed for non-EMT personnel is a great way to prepare for a disaster, while safeguarding your family on a daily basis. Topics taught during these courses focus on CPR, airway obstructions, bleeding and patient assessment. How many of you truly know how to administer CPR? I'm willing to bet the percentage barely breaks 30, and I'm feeling optimistic today!

Would it be an epic fail for the author of *The Jakarta Pandemic* to leave infectious diseases out of his first aid discussion? Probably. If you've read the novel, you pretty much know everything I know about pandemics, from the scientific side (symptoms, lethality, and transmission), to the personal management side (preventative treatment with antivirals and quarantine). The key to one hundred percent guaranteed survival during a pandemic flu is simple: *strict quarantine.* Not so simple, as I painstakingly described in my novel, but surely a manageable task if you've covered the basics and worked toward extended isolation as one of your SURVIVE WHAT scenarios.

Final word on the topic. Conventional medical supplies won't last forever in the Big Kahuna scenario. Grid down, societal collapse—call it what you will. At some point, we'll have to turn to old remedies and Mother Nature to treat illness and injury. I'm not suggesting that you turn your cheek on ibuprofen and Benadryl, but it couldn't hurt to explore some naturopathic options while you still have the luxury of experimenting. You don't have to grow your hair long, quit showering and wear tie-dye shirts to enter a natural foods store—though a few piercings and visible tattoos might help you blend in. Just kidding. Seriously, we've discovered some great "supplements" that have multiple uses beyond fostering health. Most of these are derived from plants you can grow in your backyard or on a sunny windowsill. *Oreganol (Oil of oregano) and Elderberry syrup are great places to start. Check it out.* Great knowledge to have after you pop that last pill.

Randall

Have you ever had an accident? A knife slips while you're carving a pumpkin and slices your hand open. You trip on a step carrying the laundry upstairs and fall and break a collarbone. Maybe it didn't go down exactly like that for you, but we've all had accidents where we wound up a bit worse for wear. Thankfully a trip to the emergency room is just a car ride away in most cases. Maybe it's a couple of needle sticks, and bing-bang-boom you're as good as new. But what if that wasn't how it played out? If secondary care wasn't available or you couldn't get to the hospital for some reason and you had to deal with the problem yourself, would you be able to render aid to yourself or someone else? In an emergency situation, you might find yourself in just that scenario, and how it plays out will depend solely on you.

Being the first responder of last resort is not a position any of us wants to be in, but there are things you can do to be ready. Like most things in life, education and training are a great place to start. Taking a class in basic first aid and CPR (cardiopulmonary resuscitation) should be the minimum necessary for anyone to meet the requirements of a well-thought-out preparedness plan, but we would encourage you to pursue any additional and more advanced first aid skills you may like to acquire. Now, I am not a medical professional, and nothing you read in this essay should be considered to be expert medical opinion, but I do take my own advice. Does everyone in my household know basic first aid? Yep. Have we taken a CPR class? You betcha. The skills you gain from taking basic first aid and CPR classes will cover a great percentage of what you would need to know to stabilize a victim, buying you time to seek secondary treatment or figure out your next plan of action.

So you've made the practical choice to learn some basic first aid skills. Now you need to give yourself the tactical advantage of having a well-stocked first aid kit on hand. This will make you most effective at rendering emergency first aid. Although having something is always better than having nothing, we suggest you build your own first aid kit rather than buying some pre-form kit for a couple of reasons. First, no one knows your situation better than you. In addition to all of the basic supplies you may find in a first aid kit, by crafting your own kit you can make choices about the quality of the supplies available to you and you can make key additions to the kit like an EpiPen or specific medications that you will not find in any off-the-shelf kit. Secondly, you will know what's in your kit! A shockingly obvious concept, I know, but simply buying a first aid kit and stashing it away leads you down that dark road where complacency allows you to believe that just throwing money at a problem will solve it, and that is a dangerous assumption to make. I'm willing to bet that your life or the lives of your family or members of your group are worth much more than that.

Think back to the Practical Tactical Preparedness Prism and the Cycle. There is no greater example of how important it is to understand what's in your kit and how to use it than when dealing with first aid. When life and death may literally hinge on the skills and supplies you have at your disposal in a disaster situation, I would certainly think that you would want to know exactly what is in your kit and that your skills are up to date. Another process held over from the Cycle is the kit to fit concept, and it absolutely holds true when it comes to first aid. Regardless of whether we are talking about your home, your car or the gear you carry on your person every day, you can kit to fit your first aid supplies so that you will never be without the options necessary to render assistance should the situation call for it.

Outside of the textbooks and classes, there are those "home remedies" that we've all heard before. You may know them as "old wives' tales" or something else. On that topic, I will simply say this. Don't trust all of those "home remedies" just because someone told you they will work. Trust your training. You are going to get training, right? I'm not saying that none of them have merit, but I am saying that you should investigate and explore any of these "home remedies" before using them. If you prefer a more natural approach, herbal remedies are also a consideration. Just make certain you educate yourself on this topic before taking chances with your health.

As I said, I am not a medical professional, and nothing you read in this essay should be considered to be expert medical opinion.

However, I do know several medical professionals, and I trust them implicitly. I value their opinion because it is based on years of field experience, so I asked them if they had any "inside tips" on first aid that they would like to share with the class. Here are a few things to keep in mind from the pros.

• Can you deliver the package? Keep transportation in mind. You may have the emergency first aid part of the equation covered, but have you given any thought to how you might move a severely injured patient to secondary care after you have stabilized them or whether you have the ability to contact emergency services so they can come to you?

• Have you considered personal protective equipment/body substance isolation? Before you can help someone else, you need to make sure you have taken the steps necessary to protect yourself from possible contamination from diseases transmitted via bodily fluids. Whether you choose to render aid (to a stranger) is a personal choice, but if you believe you would, why not do it safely?

• Survey the scene! Situational awareness, anyone? You cannot help anyone if you become a victim too, so make sure the scene is safe before you attempt to render aid.

• Observation is one of the most overlooked and important skills you can have as a first responder. Slow down and really look as you make your patient assessment. Assuming the injury is not completely obvious, this will help you quickly narrow your choices as you determine the source of the problem. If the injury does seem obvious, keen observation will help you verify that what appears to be the main threat actually is the most pressing health issue.

- Remember the ABCs of first aid…airway, breathing and circulation. Check to make sure that the airway is not compromised, that the patient is breathing, and that there is good circulation (do they have a pulse?).

- Do you have a clean bed sheet in your first aid kit? Add one now. A simple sheet will become the 550 parachute cord of your kit because it has so many practical uses like an emergency stretcher, a sling, you can use it to stop bleeding, treat shock, as a cold compress to treat hyperthermia, improvised feminine hygiene products, tourniquets…the list goes on. Put a clean sheet in a sturdy freezer bag and add it to your kit today.

- See the whole picture, and first, do no harm. For example, a patient has a broken arm. Instead of trying to "set" the broken arm, which risks making a bad situation worse, check for a pulse below (beyond) the break. If the pulse is strong, stabilize the break and seek secondary care if available. If the pulse is weak, it is possible there may be internal bleeding or some more imminent threat to life than the broken arm, and that will dictate your next move.

- First aid matters, and it saves lives. This is one area of your preparedness plan that you cannot afford to neglect. Get the training you need, build your own kits, and practice your skills. None of us want to ever have to use those skills, but if the situation arises that you are the first responder of last resort, you will certainly be thankful that you were prepared.

Chapter 13: SANITATION

Alex hadn't thought about the cottage's sanitary situation. Most septic systems are designed to accommodate the expected purpose of the dwelling. He couldn't imagine the builders had anticipated 17 people using the small lake house indefinitely. Even without the addition of the Fletcher's, they'd be lucky if the system survived the winter. Life on Great Pond in Belgrade would degrade fairly quickly without the use of an indoor bathroom. Another reason they were better off elsewhere. He had to be practical about this decision, and 17 people crammed into a 800 square foot cottage designed primarily for three-season use was far from practical.

—From *Point of Crisis*

Randall

The body's business breaks for no one. It doesn't matter the time of day, where you're at or what's going on. There are those times when the human body absolutely demands our attention, and we must heed the call. The call of nature, that is. Recognizing this fact of life is all that is required to understand the importance of proper sanitation. However, a good sanitation plan involves more than just covering your private business. Everything necessary to maintain good personal hygiene during a disaster should have a place in a well-rounded preparedness plan, and adequately addressing this need will require you to take a hard look at every aspect of your preparations.

On a basic level, cleanliness is at the core of everything you do now and will take on even more importance during a disaster situation. If you are dealing with an emergency, the last thing you want to have to worry about is sickness or infection brought on by an inability to remain clean. Whether it is food preparation, treating an open wound so it doesn't become infected, or keeping your waste from contaminating your drinking water, proper sanitation is paramount. If you're on the move, one of the quickest ways to be rendered ineffective is to ignore personal hygiene. A failure to keep clean can lead to bacteria growth in all of those dark, damp and steamy places on the human body, and that can lead to a painful rash or infection. If you've ever had a case of athlete's foot or a bad heat rash, you know all too well how quickly unchecked bacteria can ruin your day.

What would be your plan if the toilets don't flush due to a disruption in water service? Do you keep enough "extra" water, "extra" meaning water that is not already designated for drinking, on hand to simply flush it away? According to the Environmental Protection Agency (EPA) WaterSense website, standard toilets use 1.6 gallons per flush, while older toilets can use as much as 3.5 to 7 gallons per flush. Whichever figures you use, that's a lot of "extra" water.

There are other things you can do to meet your sanitation needs, and they don't have to be expensive. It's easy enough to make an emergency toilet using a five-gallon bucket and trash bags filled with kitty litter, or you could simply dig a latrine. Whatever you do, *don't forget the toilet paper*. If you have built it into your planning, you can have stored water for (restricted) washing or you could choose to simply use sanitary wipes and hand sanitizer to keep things clean.

Whatever methods you choose to employ when it comes to personal cleanliness and basic sanitation, just don't forget to address it. Your method doesn't have to be complicated, but it has to work. Keep things simple, separate and consistent, and odds are you will be just fine. *Just don't forget the toilet paper.*

Steven

Remember Bob? Like it or not, we need to talk about what Bob was doing on his dock. Don't worry, I'm not going to put my writing skills to the test and recreate the scene for you in vivid, first person point of view. There's no way to "sugarcoat" this subject—I know, that sounded gross. Bottom line: If the electrical grid fails for an extended period of time or your toilets are shot to pieces by a rogue militia group (happened to the Fletchers in *Event Horizon*), things will get disgusting and unsanitary really fast if you don't have a plan. And the topic of sanitation extends well beyond Bob's activities "On Golden Brown Pond." I couldn't resist that. If you survive the next few paragraphs, we'll talk about personal hygiene and trash removal.

I'll go out on a limb and say that personal waste disposal is the most overlooked topic in "prepping." Maybe we don't want to talk about it, or even think about it, because it's thoroughly unpleasant on every level. I also wonder if it's overlooked because we more or less take toilets for granted. Let's face it, the empty toilet paper roll is about the biggest sanitation challenge you and I face in our lives. If you have kids or an adult male living in your home, you might face that awkward situation a few times a month. Nobody likes to beg for toilet paper to be rolled into the bathroom like a grenade. That's why my wife generally bans us from "her" bathroom.

You might be asking yourself: Why would the toilets stop? How can it get that bad? Good questions. Before researching our water distribution system for *The Jakarta Pandemic*, I thought our pressure was solely maintained by water towers. In many cases this is true. Hydrostatic pressure (we're going to learn something!) is used in many municipalities to pressurize residential water and store emergency firefighting water. Sounds pretty basic and EMP-proof to me—except there's a catch.

The tower is constantly refilled by a pump managed by remote sensors. Without power, the tower will slowly drain and never refill—good-bye water pressure. If you don't see any towers in your town, you're not off the hook. Actually, you're worse off than the people with towers. Your water is pressurized and delivered to your house by pumping stations. You can probably guess the rest.

How long until the water stops running? Estimates vary. Some county and city distribution systems have backup power supplies designed to maintain pressure during a short outage. Water towers should give you a few more hours, if not days, depending on demand. If your house draws water from an electrically pumped well, you lose running water immediately.

All this to say: ***Your toilet draws water from the municipal supply (or well). No more water, no more flushing—without manually filling the tank from another source.***

I can fill the tank? Sounds like we're still in business. Maybe. The men reading this know how many gallons a urinal at the airport uses. 1 gallon or 3.8 liters. Thank you Toto or Kohler for that useful English to metric conversion stamped right into the porcelain. Your standard home toilet, if it's relatively new, uses 1.6 gallons per flush. ***You better not fill that up using your fresh water supply.*** This is where living on a lake or next to a stream might come in handy, or a fifty-gallon plastic barrel connected to a rain gutter. Labor intensive, but worth the hassle.

Most of us don't live near a ready supply of water or in an area with predictable rainfall, so our options will be limited—and the bad news doesn't end there. Sewage treatment plants run on electricity, and sewer systems often rely on a nearby pump station to move sewage from a gravity-fed collection point to the treatment plant. Eventually that system will back up to your street, and you won't be able to flush the toilet. Even more frightening, the sewage could back up into your house. Your home may be equipped with a sewer check valve, which will prevent this—not a bad thing to verify and install if missing.

I bet that septic system doesn't sound so "rustic" and "country" at this point. With a nearby lake, septic system and the will to haul water, your biggest sanitation nightmare might remain the dreaded empty toilet paper roll. While we're on the topic of toilet paper, let's talk about supplies and a few solutions for the vast majority of folks without waterside property and a septic system.

TOILET PAPER! How many rolls do you have right now? A one- to two-week supply—unless you just hit Costco. Don't we all pray that the apocalypse will happen (if it has to happen) after the big Costco run? Don't count on it. You need more toilet paper on hand. It doesn't "go bad," so you can buy a few Big Kahuna packages and stuff them in the corner of your basement (as long as the basement doesn't flood) with a "Use only in emergency" sign. Seriously. I don't expect you to buy a year's worth of TP. Keep in mind: SURVIVE WHAT? Start there and expand your supply a little further. You won't regret it.

What happens to that TP if you have to bug out? If you're travelling by car, I suggest you stuff as much as possible in the nooks and crannies. You can flatten the roll into an oval and jam it in pretty tight places. The paper still functions—that's all that counts. If you're on foot, it gets a little trickier. Obviously, you can't carry the forty-roll superpack with you. When I went into the field with the marines, I carried two flattened rolls in a Ziploc bag, along with a container of baby wipes. This sounds like a reasonable load-out for your BOLT kit.

Oh, the glorious baby wipe. Man and woman's best friend when the water stops flowing. Baby wipes serve two purposes. A clean underside wipe and convenient way to wash your hands and face. Not with the same wipe, please. I consider these an indispensable sanitation item for situations where soap and water are not readily available. Like the toilet paper, you can compact these (take the refillable bag out of the hard plastic shell) and stuff them everywhere. Soap? Is it uncool to use soap in the field? Only the marines would hassle you for that. A bar of soap (or body wash) and a bottle of shampoo is an essential addition to your family's BOLT kit. You might consider adding a few bottles to your personal readiness stockpile at home.

I think I got ahead of myself on this topic. We've talked a lot about wiping, but little about "the main event." What can I say? Lots of options. None of them great. Alex Fletcher bought four sizable buckets and a ton of kitchen waste bags (the kind with the drawstrings). When I wrote that scene, I envisioned those sturdy, white five-gallon buckets. You can sit on those. That's the most rudimentary "I don't want to dig a hole in the backyard" option. The technology gets better. Camping toilets are available. I've seen portable and flushable variations for $90. You still have to dump those at some point, but it kind of works on the same principle as the "porta potties" you see at the county fair—without the stifling heat and flies. Like I said a little earlier, these are indoor options. The best solution is an outdoor system, which gets the waste out of your living quarters. You'll have to take weather, security and ground water contamination (well) into account. I'll let you research makeshift outhouses on your own—I'm about to have lunch.

Let's move to a less stomach-wrenching topic—personal hygiene. I'll keep this simple. ***Don't give up. To stay human, you need to feel somewhat human.*** Brush your teeth like normal. Cut your nails. Clean your body and hair as best as possible given the circumstances. If that means wiping your face, hands, armpits and nether regions with a few baby wipes—so be it! You got the basics covered. Not enough? You can bathe outdoors if the area is safe. Don't waste your time staring at the showerhead wistfully. Those days are gone—for now. Think about the Irish Spring commercial.

Your experience might not be as robust or cheerful, but dumping a bucket of somewhat fresh water over your head, lathering up and dumping a few more buckets to rinse off will make all the difference. Just make sure Bob isn't sitting on the dock when you take your natural shower—and keep your eyes and mouth closed.

Last but not least, what will you do with all of that trash? My guess is you'll have less and less trash as time progresses. In the early stages of a disaster or prolonged crisis, your family may still generate a significant amount of garbage. The volume will decrease rapidly as no more packaging or "throw away" food is brought into the house. I find that packaging comprises at least 95% of our garbage. In the summer, when my family gets serious about composting and eat out of the garden, we barely fill a single kitchen trash bag.

I'm torn on what to recommend for WHERE to store it. Trash invites pests, so you really don't want to keep bags in the house. Trash also invites curious people, especially when they're hungry, so placing your bags away from the house might lead to the discovery that you're still eating two months into complete shutdown of the food distribution system. Congratulations, you just appeared on everyone's radar screen! I think the garage might be a smart compromise.

Did I really spend that much time on SANITATION? It wasn't a mistake. Now I need to run out and hit the store, because I believe in practicing what I preach—and we've got about a week's worth of TP between three bathrooms.

Chapter 14: GROUNDING YOURSELF

Ryan tugged Chloe's hand to force her along. Progress across the exposed intersection had been stop and go since the shooting started. She had dropped to the mud several times during their trek across the exposed intersection, the crack and hiss of near misses short-circuiting her legs. He just needed to get her behind the Jersey barrier and out of immediate danger. Ryan slid his right arm under her left arm and shoved her forward, pushing against her back. Bullets ricocheted off the barrier in front of them as they edged toward the temporary reprieve of the one-foot-thick, steel-reinforced concrete barricade.

She sank to the pavement behind the wall, placing her back against the concrete and burying her face in her knees. Her body twitched uncontrollably, and Ryan couldn't tell if she was hyperventilating or crying. He pressed his forehead against her pink ball cap and held her tightly, wishing he could soothe her. The maelstrom of incoming fire intensified, showering them with concrete fragments. Chloe flinched at every sound. There was nothing he could do for her right now, other than get her to the other side of the bridge.

—From *Event Horizon*

Steven

When Randy suggested this chapter, I thought, for the first time ever, that I would have nothing to say. We talk about the tangible elements of readiness—plans, gear, redundancy and resilience—but we rarely speak about psychological preparedness. How do you do that anyway? You can train your body with pull-ups, sit-ups, jogging, hiking, walking, just getting off the couch or eating different foods—it's fairly easy to shrink our physical comfort zone. Most of us avoid it, but it's within our grasp, and we have a lifetime of experience making choices that test some of our limits. We wear inadequate clothing in cold weather. We diet and feel hungry. We exercise until we can barely stand up. Jump in cold water. The list is endless. I'm not suggesting you and I are ready to join the next SEAL training class, but we've been around the block a few times when it comes to physical challenges. It's not a foreign concept.

How do you cultivate mental toughness for a disaster or your SURVIVE WHAT scenario? There's no roadmap for this. I'm not going to say, "You either have it or you don't." I wholeheartedly do not believe that. Without a doubt, some of us (not saying me) start out with more mental toughness than others. The old nature versus nurture argument. Mental toughness can be developed, but it takes a long time. I think it's fair to say that we're working with a limited time frame and need a few quicker-to-access strategies.

One of the most powerful mental tools you can harness is **PURPOSE or MISSION.** Let the reason you have decided to embark on the preparedness journey be your mantra. Alex's purpose was to "protect his family." EVERY action he took served this purpose and provided a FOCUS. A focal point is the same as a grounding point. It serves as a lens to simplify your actions and reactions to a situation, whether it's choosing the next item to purchase for your readiness plan or reacting to a threat.

Taking FOCUS one step further, I'd like to introduce you to the concept of Mental Rehearsal or, as I like to call it, "focused daydreaming." Oh, boy. Konkoly was pushing it with the last suggestion. Now he wants me to sit at work and daydream about the apocalypse? Not exactly. I write books based on "what if" scenarios I've imagined far from the keyboard. The books you've read barely scratch the surface of the scenarios I've conceived, shopping at the grocery store, eating with my family, driving around town, flying in an airplane—everywhere. I don't walk around with a vacant look on my face, miles away in my head. I'm just subconsciously mulling over "what I might do if something happened."

Is it fair to say that most of what you've read in *The Jakarta Pandemic* and *The Perseid Collapse* series felt realistic or plausible for the character? There's nothing stopping you from being the star of your own survival novel, on a more limited scale. Sounds a little crazy, but I'm not making this up.

Mental rehearsal is a valid strategy employed by elite military forces (seriously—you can research this), and it's available to everyone, free of charge. I bet you like the sound of that—I know your significant other does. We've all *mentally rehearsed* spending a year's salary to arrive at this chapter. Mental rehearsal is simple. ***You visualize success in a realistic task or scenario, over and over again.*** This can be applied to every aspect of your preparedness plan, including your reaction to the event. Are you going to freak out when the tsunami siren sounds? No. You're going to calmly but forcefully direct your family to grab their BOLT kits and load the car within three minutes. After that, I don't care if the scene in your head resembles something out of the latest disaster movie, with your car speeding ahead of the destruction. As long as your plan succeeds in a realistic fashion, you're on the right path.

The lawyers are tapping me on the shoulder. Disclaimer time. No matter how many times I visualize jumping out of my car on the freeway (at 70 mph) and landing perfectly on my feet, it's not gonna happen that way. My feet may hit at the same time, but I will quickly go into a tumble that will most assuredly end in my death. The key to mental rehearsal is pick a ***realistic task or scenario***. Please don't forget SURVIVE WHAT? You shouldn't be driving around rehearsing the zombie apocalypse—like I do. Hey, I can get away with it. I do this for a living.

Randall

Preparing for a disaster does not have to mean you are preparing for the end of the world or even the end of the world as we know it as a result of some event like a total societal collapse. To our way of thinking, if you are preparing for events that would constitute a disaster on a personal scale, then you are going about things the right way. With that said, it is the personal impacts of any disaster that often prove to be the most debilitating, and these impacts often determine whether we will ultimately pull through in difficult times. Even if the reasons for practicing a preparedness lifestyle can be completely different in every way from focus to scale, there is still one facet of preparedness that is common to every situation and is vitally important.

One of the key factors in survival and therefore in preparedness is the ability to remain in a good head space, to keep a positive outlook regardless of the situation, and to have the mental toughness to choose to keep moving forward. To put it another way, everyone has a method of "finding their center" or pulling themselves together in the middle of the storm. We all get shaken from time to time, but the ability to regain focus is what sets the survivor apart from the rest. Whether it is a personal spirituality or faith, a set of skills gained through training, or strength and motivation gained from our personal relationships, we all have some way of pulling ourselves together when times are tough. Identifying what keeps you grounded in your personal life before you are faced with disaster is the key to your survival mindset and is a powerful preparedness technique that will give you clarity of purpose and put you miles ahead in your journey to preparedness.

Knowing what forms the foundation of your emotional self is invaluable, but there is still more you can do to strengthen your psychological resilience, apocalypse or not. At every level of your preparedness planning, we recommend that you build comfort items into the kits of each member of your family or group. "Comfort items" are exactly what you might think they are, items that bring comfort to their owner or the person carrying them. Whether it's a case of chocolate bars or a pound of quality coffee added to your food storage, a favorite toy or book added to a child's BOLT kit, or a treasured picture kept in your everyday carry gear, these items can have an extremely powerful impact on their respective owners. This is one of those instances when it really is the little things that matter.

"If you can keep your head when all about you
Are losing theirs and blaming it on you,
If you can trust yourself when all men doubt you,
But make allowance for their doubting too; ..."
~ excerpt from Rudyard Kipling's *"If"*

Disaster strikes, rocking you out of your comfort zone and turning your world upside down. What's next? It all starts between the ears. I am not the first to say that the human mind is the greatest survival tool you will ever have at your disposal, and I have no hesitation adding my voice to the chorus of those who have said the same before me. Regardless of the level of disaster you are faced with, it is crucial to maintain the ability to shake off the shock of the event and get yourself back in the game and your family or group focused and moving forward. If you can strengthen your psychological resilience by simply adding a comfort item to your kit, that is certainly a practical and tactical move that I believe you should make.

Chapter 15: SURVIVAL TEAM DISASTER PLAN

Just thinking about Alex's transmission energized him. By now, Alex should have reached Ryan's dorm room. Everything depended on what he found there. Ryan was supposed to travel to Chloe's apartment in the event of an emergency, where they'd wait for their parents. He desperately needed to hear that Ryan wasn't in his room. It meant that Chloe was safe. He knew the discovery would be tough on Alex, but it represented the best chance that both of them were safe.

—From *The Perseid Collapse*

Randall

Growing up, I was a lucky kid. Not only did I have the extremely good fortune of growing up in a safe and loving home with two parents and a large community of people that genuinely cared about my brother and I, we also had the "cool" parents. No, really. My parents actually were very cool. We had a great time together. My brother and I got to stay up later than most children, experience all of the awesome things life has to offer (that were age appropriate) and my parents had a great sense of humor. They were a ton of fun. It wasn't all fun and games, though. Mom and Dad had no patience for genuinely stupid activities that would get somebody hurt or anything that involved unnecessary risk in pursuit of some mythical glory, and when it came to disaster planning, there was no fooling around.

For our family, preparedness started at home. We lived in several different places when I was a kid, but one of the very first things we learned after moving into a new location was how to evacuate that structure in case of emergency and where to meet back up as a family. A fire was usually the fictitious scenario that would force us from our rooms in the middle of the night, and the most popular meeting place was across the street at a mailbox or a large tree. The rules were pretty simple:

1. Get out!
2. Get together.
3. Don't go back.

My parents kept it simple, straightforward and powerful.

Looking back on this most basic disaster planning as an adult, I have to say I approve. All these years later and it's hard to find fault with their planning or methods. Our world was simple, and they kept things that way.

Though evolved, this concept is what shaped our preparedness philosophy at Practical Tactical. In so many words:

1. Know your team (also read as family or group).
2. Know your situation.
3. Execute your plan.

You don't have to think too hard to see how the Preparedness Prism and the Cycle overlay nicely with this approach. Simple. Focused. Practical.

When you think about preparedness, it does not matter who makes up your team or survival group. It could be family, friends, neighbors...anyone. As long as you **know** you can trust the members of your team and everyone is committed to the same mission, that's usually good enough. Once you know who's on your team, you have to craft your plan based on that reality. Maybe everyone lives together, but maybe not. Maybe everyone lives in the neighborhood, but maybe not. In most cases the members of a group like this will help one another whenever the need arises, but that's not always the case. If it's not, what triggers the group's emergency action plan? All of these things and many more must be considered before any preparedness plan is to have a real chance of succeeding.

In my personal life, the same rules apply. In the case of an immediate emergency like a house fire, we have a designated meeting place away from our home but still inside the neighborhood. Should some event force us out of our neighborhood, we have designated a secondary rally point. As mentioned earlier, should disaster strike while we are away from home or at work, we have a plan to get back home. If going home is not an option for some reason and we are not together, we would head to another predetermined location to link up and reassess the situation. I think you get the point. We have game-planned scenarios at every level, have developed plans to fit each situation, and are confident in our ability to execute them.

Remember the Prism. Planning is where it all begins. Regardless of who or how many are in your group, each person and each situation must be factored into your team's plan. Think about the Cycle. Once your plan is in place, you have to put it to the test. Let's say you live in a two-story home and you have children. Do you have an emergency ladder in case of a fire, does everyone in your home know how to use it, and do they know where to go when they get out of the house? Remember, planning, purpose of use and practice. Think education, planning, kit to fit, training, and evaluation. Around and around it goes until you are certain everyone in your group knows the drill and believes it will work.

The other part of this equation is your home disaster kit. This collection of basic gear will serve as the backbone of your group disaster planning going forward. Of course, you will need to cover the basic tenets of preparedness in this kit. If you haven't already started to put this basic kit together, I would refer you to the Practical Tactical Quick Start Guide where you will find what we call the Quarter-Hour Kit. This concept lays out a quick, step-by-step process to covering each of the basic tenets of preparedness, which can then be scaled up to meet your needs at your own pace.

Trust the process and believe in your team. Taking the time to develop your disaster plans now will give everyone the best chance of seeing each other back at the big oak tree across the road later, and trust me, if you ever have to look for that big oak in the middle of some awful night, you will be so thankful you knew where to go.

Steven

Typically, this is a three-hundred-page document written in two different languages (in case you panic and forget your native tongue) and converted to audiobook (for obvious reasons—panic blindness) covering every possible disaster scenario and response you might face. You're not going to do that? Neither am I. Nobody, including the author, will ever read it again. We're not talking about a step-by-step plan for every aspect of your SURVIVE WHAT scenario. The Survival Team Disaster Plan is more of an initial "disaster response" designed to safely deliver your "survival team" to a designated area for the next steps. You can't rehearse an entire disaster, or expect everyone to have their precise roles memorized from day one to day 180, but you can surely take the time to physically or mentally rehearse the first steps.

How do you know who's in your "survival team"? The government assigns everyone to a specific group based on geography, skills and temperament. Your team number and contact information is provided on your annual social security statement—JUST KIDDING! Did anyone start panicking? Sorry, I can't resist doing that. "Survival team" is just a fancy term for the people (and pets) covered by your readiness plan. Immediate family, elderly parents one town over, neighbors or friends—***whoever's going into the bunker with you.***

Sounds easy enough, but what if the kids are in school and you're a forty-five-minute train ride away with no way to contact them (cell phones knocked out)? Do the kids stay in place and wait for you to pick them up, or do they walk home? Do the kids meet up at one of the schools? Which one? How long do they stay before attempting to reach home? What if home isn't an option due to flooding or some other kind of destruction? Not so easy anymore—and I've barely scratched the surface.

Frankly, this is my biggest nightmare. ***I've adequately prepared for my SURVIVE WHAT scenario, but I can't reach my kids and wife.*** The first two books in my latest post-apocalyptic series hinge around this fear. As you might imagine, I've devoted days of thought to this dilemma, eventually creating a basic, layered plan to address this issue. My core plan relies on predetermined Rally Points (known or easily identified geographic locations), assuming no communication will be possible. I recommend starting here, because this gives you a foundation. If cell phones work (voice or texting), you can adjust the plan to make it easier for everyone involved.

This can be hard to envision, so I'm going to create a scenario that "resembles" my own situation. Here it is.

SCENARIO:

-I have two kids in different schools in my town.
-The schools are less than a half-mile away from each other.

-We live four miles from the closest school (two main routes to reach schools).

-I work at home.

-My wife works thirty minutes south in a less congested area.

TEAM DISASTER PLAN:

1. **If the children are not in school or summer day camp:** The PRIMARY RALLY POINT is our home. I work out of the house, so I'm almost always here. When the kids aren't in school, this is our gathering point. My wife is to proceed home as quickly as possible. I will collect the kids (from friends' houses…hopefully nearby) and wait for her to arrive. She's facing a thirty-minute drive or an all-day walk. If no communications are possible, she's walking the entire way. Sounds rough, but it's far too risky to go looking for her along a thirty-miles stretch of several roads—during a crisis capable of knocking out the power. An exception will be made if I have both kids and I can talk with my wife. We'll come get her if possible. *One of the key themes found in our rules is keeping as many people together at one time as possible.*

If home is not an option for whatever reason, we'll meet at the SECONDARY RALLY POINT, which is my daughter's school. It's tucked away out of sight, near the police station, and will likely be used as a shelter in a crisis capable of forcing people out of their homes.

2. **If children are in school when a major disaster strikes:** My son leaves his school and proceeds to the SECONDARY RALLY POINT (I chose the school earlier for a reason. One set of rally points). Short of the teachers physically restraining him, he has these marching orders. I want my kids together in a significant crisis. They ride the same bus, so if bus service is offered immediately, they are both to get on the bus. If my son isn't on the bus when it arrives at my daughter's school (second pickup for the bus), she declines the ride and waits for my son to arrive on foot. Likewise, if my daughter does not get on the bus when it stops at my daughter's school, my son gets off and searches for her. My children will wait there for one of us to arrive.

If my wife or I haven't arrived within four hours, they are to proceed to the family's TERTIARY RALLY POINT, the police station half a mile away from the school. I can drive to the school in eight minutes, bike the distance in thirty minutes or less, jog it in forty-five minutes, or walk it in ninety. Unless I'm out of town, injured or taken out by a tsunami, I'll be there within four hours. If not, I want them at the police station.

My wife is the wildcard in this scenario. It would take her most of the day to walk home, assuming she could travel along the coastal roads. If car travel was not an option, she would head north, first stopping at the TERTIARY RALLY POINT (she's not walking home in four hours) to look for the kids (which is on her way HOME), then the SECONDARY RALLY POINT, just in case the kids got sent back or we all left the house. She does the same thing if she's driving. If she doesn't find us at my daughter's school or the police station, there's a good bet that we're home. ***What if we're not in any of these places?***

3. FINAL RALLY POINTS: This is a tough one, and it will vary from group to group based on geography, population and your existing social/family network. Here are a few suggested guidelines. You want to pick at least one point reachable by every member of the team—preferably on foot. This may not be possible with small children or the elderly. Adjust accordingly. I also recommend selecting a point further away for a vehicle rendezvous. However you craft this part of the plan, your FINAL RALLY POINTS need to be located in a geographically safe area (most likely to be safe).

For us, that means north (away from higher population areas) or west (away from the water). If you have family in the area, this point could be right across town or the town over. I highly recommend some geographic separation from your other rally points. The purpose of the FINAL RALLY POINT is to get you away from a likely area of danger.

Are you ready to sit down with your family and map this out? You still look a little skeptical about their response. I don't blame you. Springing a SEAL mission on them at the beginning might not be the best "buy in" strategy for your overall disaster readiness efforts. Why don't you start off with a fire drill rehearsal at the house? That's a disaster too, and should be on everyone's list of SURVIVE WHAT scenarios. After this, you can step it up to something a little more complicated, like a home intruder response drill. Have I just named two of the most likely home "disaster" scenarios that very few of you (me included) rehearse or discuss with your families? Once again, I'm not here to make you feel guilty. As I type these words, the hypocrite police are watching over my shoulder to make sure I come clean.

Bottom line: Take baby steps WITH your family or team before you graduate to a Team Disaster Plan with multiple RALLY POINTS.

Final word on this subject. Did any of you feel sorry for my wife? Thirty miles is one hell of a walk and will require some supplies. Water, food (energy bars) and appropriate clothing (including footwear) are the bare minimum. My wife sometimes wears a suit to work—that's not appropriate for a thirty-mile walk in ninety-degree weather. If your Survival Team Disaster Plan involves someone possibly travelling longer distances, you should consider a Get Home Bag (GHB). In the scenario described above, if I left my house to get the kids at school or a friend's house, I would put together a Get Home Bag to help facilitate our return. What's in a Get Home Bag beside water, food and clothing? You'll have to read the next chapter to find out.

Chapter 16: FOUNDATIONS OF PREPAREDNESS

Another thought crossed his mind, but he dismissed it. They would have been hit by the shockwave already if it was a nuke. Either way, his only mission at this point was to reach Chloe and figure out what to do next. Stay in Boston or trek north? He lifted a blue, twenty-gallon plastic storage bin from the closet floor and dropped it on his bed.

The bin had been the last item to leave the car, hidden under a blanket by his dad. Ryan had nearly refused to take it up to his room. Of the 21,000 incoming freshmen, he didn't want to be the only one with a "paranoia pack" taking up precious space in his closet. Of course, that was the point of the bin. Boston University represented a small city of students, most of them completely dependent on the university's infrastructure for their basic survival needs. With his mom in tears over dropping him off at college, he decided to take it and spare her the worry. Based on what he had experienced over the last few minutes, Ryan was fairly certain that the university's infrastructure had ceased to exist. The emergency bin didn't sound so ridiculous anymore.

The container held an olive green backpack, two CamelBak water bladders and a sealed plastic bucket of dehydrated food pouches. The backpack had been outfitted with enough gear and food to support a two-day journey. Each of the bladders held three liters, which was the theoretical minimum he should drink per day if hiking. Realistically, he'd need more, which was why his dad had stuffed a Katadyn microfilter into the backpack. His first task upon leaving the dorm room was to fill both of the CamelBak bladders. Beyond that, everything he needed to walk back to Maine with Chloe was inside the backpack.

The pack contained a hat, old sunglasses, maps of Boston and New England, a compass, extra cash, parachute cord, a thirty-foot section of remnant sailing line, a small emergency radio, first aid kit, fire-starting kit, flashlight, three MREs, a Gore-Tex bivouac bag, N95 respirator and an emergency blanket. The only thing he didn't have was a knife. Any knife, no matter how small, was classified as a weapon by university police and strictly forbidden. Even a Swiss Army knife could get you expelled. He dug through one of the outer pouches and found the flashlight. He aimed the LED light at the window and tested it, relieved that it filled the entire room with a bluish-white light. He had no idea what kind of damage a solar flare could do to battery-powered equipment.

He considered unpacking the dehydrated food bucket, but there was no way he could stuff anything else into the backpack. The bucket would be awkward to carry, but it had a sturdy handle, and he wasn't going far enough for it to become a real problem. He'd cover the three miles to Chloe's apartment in thirty minutes. Forty tops. He heaved the backpack onto his shoulders and tightened the straps. With the bucket in his left hand, he leaned against the door and listened. The screaming had faded to sporadic yelling.

—From *Event Horizon*

Randall

As we've already mentioned, practicing personal preparedness and living a readiness lifestyle builds resilience into your daily life and acts as a type of insurance for your family or group against the very real and common disaster threats that we all live with every day. This will afford you the opportunity to mitigate any of the possible impacts from some potential future disaster on your team.

At this point, you should have a clear understanding of the importance of planning to any preparedness playbook. Finally, it's time to talk a bit about the fun stuff and dig into some of that "tacti-cool" gear, or the tools in your toolbox, that will essentially serve as your shield against the threats you may face in a disaster or emergency situation. So my fellow process wonks do not fear, we're not done with planning and set up just yet.

As part of the Practical Tactical holistic approach to preparedness planning, we believe in an all encompassing and well rounded strategy that will provide you with a system of gear, wrapped around a framework of solid planning that will provide support and options for your family or group at every level and in any situation. The first level of readiness is tied to the idea that we all would like to stay at home if possible during any disaster or emergency situation and is built around your group's basic disaster plan and primary or home disaster kit.

Disaster does not care about the clock or what is convenient for your schedule, so you must be prepared to respond at all times and in all situations. As an acknowledgement to this reality, it is prudent to have a plan of attack should events conspire to force you out of your home.

This is where the Practical Tactical BOLT kit comes into play. Your BOLT kit is a mobile emergency kit that is put together using the basic tenets of preparedness (shelter, water, food, fire, communications and defense, and psychology) as a guide that will allow you to maintain a level of basic operations for a limited time as you *BOLT* to your next location according to your preparedness plan that will hopefully be your safe haven from the immediate threat.

Practical Tactical B.O.L.T. Kit: What it is and what it's for

You've probably heard of a Bug Out Bag (BOB) or a Get Out Of Dodge (GOOD) bag that can be used as a grab and go kit in case you have to leave an area during an emergency situation. At Practical Tactical, we urge our clients to build what we call a BOLT (Basic Operations for a Limited Time) Kit.

Now, what makes our BOLT Kit any different from every other Bug Out or GOOD Bag out there? A focused philosophy, that's what. Often when people talk about emergency bags (regardless of what you call them) the idea starts out the same…put together a bag of essential items like food and water in case you have to leave in a hurry because of an emergency that will help you survive the event…simple, right? But from there, things tend to spin out and become ever more nebulous. Inevitably you end with *Jack the Survivor* strapping a pack to his back that contains everything from his favorite comic books to ammo for his Barrett 50 cal. which by the way, he has lovingly cradled in his arms as he treks into the wilderness to live off the land for the duration of the apocalypse, and if you don't do that too you're doomed to fail miserably and die immediately or be swallowed up by the very mindless hordes you were trying to escape in the first place.

Whew! That was *exhausting.*

The point is this. With so many variables involved in any possible future evacuation scenario, it is very easy to quickly become overwhelmed and intimidated simply by the thought of it all. Nobody wants to leave their home, but the SHTF every day for someone and you never know when you might be the one standing in front of the fan. So why not face reality and prepare yourself as best you can to be able to meet the challenge should it ever come knocking at your door at 4 am on some random Tuesday night by taking a focused approach to the task at hand, and that's getting you and your family out of harms way in the quickest and most efficient way possible.

At Practical Tactical, we believe in developing a plan in advance of the chaos that will keep you from becoming a refugee should you ever have to leave your home due to an emergency. We think of it as the *software* to go along with the *hardware* (read as gear) of preparedness. If you leave you home or primary residence without a definite destination and a well thought out and practiced plan on how to get there, you have instantly become a refugee and that's a bad spot to be in. During a time of crisis, history has shown us that the life of a refugee is cold, hard and short. Whatever you do, you do not want to become a refugee.

Now, if you have grown up in the woods and have years of experience living off the land out there and that is the *plan* you choose to craft, kit and employ, that's fine. But let's be honest, that's not most people. And that's okay. Developing a plan that calls for you to relocate to another more "permanent" location is just as viable an alternative, but must be crafted, kitted out and employed just the same. Where you go, what you do and how you do it are all parts to this formula that each of us must decide for ourselves. Be it another piece of land that you own or if you have planned ahead of time to go to a friend or relative's home outside the impacted area, in our view a definite destination point is vital and that is where a thought out and well built BOLT kit comes in to play.

For a basic explanation of the BOLT Kit, we turn to the Practical Tactical Quick Start Guide. Keep in mind that the list you will find below should be considered a starting point and is in no way the end-all-be-all of mobile emergency kits, nor should it be viewed that way. It is simply our goal to get you to think a little differently about what it means to have to evacuate and how to best develop your plans going forward.

BOLT Kit (72+ hrs as you go from point A to point B)

Bugging out (BOB), getting out of Dodge (GOOD), emergency evacuation....they all mean essentially the same thing. Something's gone down in your area, it is no longer safe for you to stay there and you have to leave your home in a hurry. This is counterintuitive in every way for most of us. Your home is your safe place. None of us would make this option our first choice, but that doesn't mean some situation might arise that will force us out and that is why we strongly suggest you have a BOLT Kit prepped and ready to go for each member of your household. This mobile kit will allow you to maintain your Basic Operations for a Limited Time as you BOLT to your next location that will hopefully be your safe haven from the immediate threat. We cannot control when, where or how disaster will strike, but we can control how prepared we are to deal with disaster. There is a fine line between order and chaos and sometimes that line can be measured in seconds. When every second counts, having a plan and the tools to see that plan through are crucial to survival. As the name implies, your BOLT Kit is the tactical advantage that will help get you through and past any emergency situation.

PRACTICAL APPLICATION:

Natural disasters
- **Hurricane**
- **Tornado**
- **Flooding**
- **Winter storms**
- **Earthquake**

Fire (wildfires, neighboring buildings)
Extended power outage
Chemical spill
Infrastructure failure
Terrorist attack

Your BOLT Kit should be a backpack. This will allow you to keep you hands free to deal with any other challenges you might face as you put your emergency plan into effect. Your pack should be large enough and sturdy enough to carry all the gear you will need to sustain you for *at least* 72 hours of independent survival and comfortable enough to carry for long periods of time. As mentioned above, your BOLT Kit is the gear you will need, based on your plan, to get you from point A to point B and away from the immediate threat that is built by you. You can easily extend the gear in you kit to sustain you for a longer period of time if you choose to do so. Your kit should be ever-evolving and based on your needs, wants and tastes and any BOLT Kit is better than nothing at all in an emergency.

Water (1 liter/day minimum)
Water filter / purification tabs
- Three options of boiling, filtering and chemical treatment will give you flexibility in securing one of the most basic survival needs
   Stainless steel water container

Energy bars and/or other packable/portable foods
- Dehydrated camping meals
- MREs (Meals Ready to Eat)
- Canned goods or Soups
- Meal bars / Energy or Candy bars

Small cooking kit
- Small metal pot
- Spork / utensil
- Metal cup

P38 Can Opener

Lightweight backpack stove with fuel

Hiking Boots / Walking Shoes / Wool Socks

Change of clothes / Weather appropriate (rotate seasonally) and Underwear

Ear plugs / Gloves / Hat / Sunglasses

Rain gear

Military poncho (can be used as shelter)

Emergency blanket (can be used as shelter)

Waterproof rip-stop tarp (can be used as shelter)

Lightweight camping tent

Lightweight (small pack) sleeping bag (30 degree)

Fire starting capabilities (lighters, tinder, etc.)

Quality Multi-tool

Quality knife and Knife sharpener

Binoculars

Flashlight / Headlamp with extra batteries / glow sticks

First Aid kit / Insect repellent

Hygiene kit (including toilet paper)

N95 face mask / bandana / shemagh / scarf / etc.

Fully charged cell phone

Emergency radio (battery or hand crank)

Maps of local areas (pre-marked with multiple routes home) / Compass

Pen and Paper

Copies of Important documents (driver's license, social security card, account & phone numbers, medical information)

Medications (if required)

Self-Defense Items (in accordance with your local laws and personal comfort level)

Cash (stored in several places; DO NOT show all your money at one time)

Rescue signal items

200 feet Parachute cord

Duct tape

Sewing kit

Heavy duty garbage bags

So just to recap:

** Decide on a definite destination (with multiple alternatives depending on the crisis) should you ever have to leave your home

** Make a plan on how to reach those destinations

** Build a BOLT kit tailored to fit your plan and review the contents every six months

** Practice your plan before you need it

The BOLT concept can be as simple as your backpack and a plan or it can be expanded to fit any situation you can imagine. Here's a tip to keep in mind as you develop your BOLT kit and plans. Create a hard copy checklist of CANNOT FORGET items that you will want to take with you in the event you have to leave your primary residence or tasks that you must take care of before leaving your home. Attach it to a fastening system and clip it to your BOLT kit. This small move will ensure that if you can't remain at home and you must leave, at least you can leave with the peace of mind that you've given yourself and your family or group every opportunity to remain safe and that is, after all, the top priority.

The concept that gives you the ability to fit your kit to the scale you need it to be to meet your preparedness goals is central to the Practical Tactical philosophy. We've discussed the home disaster kit and the BOLT kit, but a complete preparedness plan does not end there for most people. If you're in a situation like ours, the daily commute to work is a part of life for my wife and I and we have to plan for the realities that presents. The answer to this problem is the Get Home Bag (GHB), which is essentially a scaled down version of our BOLT kits, that we keep in our vehicles at all times. A good GHB is put together the same way as you would build a BOLT kit, covers the same basic needs, but serves a different purpose because it is based on a different situation. Instead of leaving your home or primary residence, the goal of a GHB is to get you back to your home and the rest of your preparedness supplies and team. Beyond the GHB, there is a more personal set of gear known as an Every Day Carry (EDC) kit. This collection of gear is made up of the stuff you keep with you, either in a small bag or on your person, at all times. Just like the GHB, your EDC will cover all of your basic preparedness needs albeit in a different way and on a smaller scale. For further explanation of the kits mentioned here including lists of suggested gear, check out the Quick Start Guide.

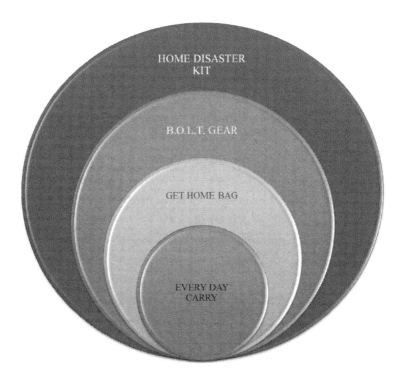

While we're discussing purpose specific kits, I would be remiss if I didn't remind you to consider your pets in your preparedness planning. *Don't forget Fido!* If you have pets and you consider them a part of your family, then of course you will want to do all you can to take care of them in a disaster. Regardless of what type of pet you have, you can build specific supplies into your home disaster kit with them in mind or even put together a BOLT kit of sorts for them. Think about the same basic things you will think about for yourself like food and water and add those items to your kits. If you have a dog that's big enough, your pet can even carry his own gear in a pack that's made for him. Our pets want to be wherever we are and we would never leave them behind, so it only makes sense to make sure we include them into our preparedness plans.

The underlying idea of our *Kit to Fit* concept is to establish a foundation of personal preparedness throughout every area of your life. There is a certain amount of overlap built into this method of planning, but that is by design for a couple of reasons. Obviously, the primary benefit is this method builds resilience into your plans through a redundancy of gear and this is always a good plan of action. To our way of thinking, if something is important enough to warrant consideration in your preparedness planning, then it is certainly important enough to earn a back up plan. Secondly, think back to chapter 5 where we discussed framing the basics. Just because there is an overlap in planning across your various kits does not mean that you have to accomplish each individual goal with the same piece of gear. This method does not only raise your overall level of resilience, it also builds options into each of your preparedness plans and that allows for flexibility. As we learned in the early chapters, being flexible and having the ability to adjust to a rapidly changing situation on the fly is often the difference between who is counted as a survivor and who ends up a statistic. Do the work of laying a solid foundation of preparedness today and give yourself and your group every chance to walk away a survivor.

Steven

Randy says BOLT kit. You say Bug Out Bag. I say potato. You say potato. How many of you pronounced the second "potato" differently? Just curious. No matter what you call this kit, it forms one of the pillars of your disaster readiness plan. By this point, it shouldn't come as a surprise to anyone that disasters don't discriminate when it comes to handing down a verdict. You can have the most meticulously crafted survival plan in the entire state, including solar panels, automated sentry turrets (not recommended for the suburbs), twenty years of dehydrated food. EVERYTHING covered—and good old Mother Nature decides it's time for that "once every hundred years" flood to sweep over the riverbanks a few blocks away, or for the Santa Ana winds to kick up early in the season and fan the flames of a brushfire toward your subdivision. It could be something as simple as a tree falling through your roof during a storm. No matter how much time, effort and money you put into your HOME, you need to prepare for an unplanned, immediate departure.

I purposely put Randy's essay first in this chapter, because he's put an incredible amount of time and thought into the BOLT kit. Basic Operations for a Limited Time. There's probably not much left to say about the kit itself, so I'll focus on other aspects of BOLTing.

Not every disaster scenario will require you to announce, "We leave in three minutes!" You should be prepared for that possibility (seriously), but don't feel like you have to limit your "Bug Out" plan to a single, stuffed backpack to toss in your car at the last second. Build the BOLT kit Randy described first, as your foundation, and consider expanding the concept in layers. In the water chapter, I mentioned that we keep several 2.5-gallon jugs of water in the garage at all times. This is part of our expanded BOLT plan—if we have the option of using a car.

In addition to water, I keep a fifty-gallon plastic bin in the basement, which is filled with portable food, camping gear, a bigger tent, tools, propane canisters, cooking equipment—it's basically an extended BOLT kit designed for a longer term, self-sufficient trip to safety. Two people can haul that out of our bulkhead door and into the back of one of our vehicles in less than a minute. This does not replace our individual BOLT backpacks— these go in the car too. If the car breaks down, you're back to the 72-hour bag, plus whatever you're willing to haul on foot from the trunk of the car.

Beyond the plastic bin in my basement, you'll find a few empty milk crates near the canned and dry food. If we have the time, we'll load up as much of our stored food (or other supplies) as possible into these crates and slide them into the car (or cars). I have a rooftop carrier for one of the vehicles, which adds eleven cubic feet of additional storage. This is not an item I will attempt to install in a hurry, but it's an option. Some of you might own small utility trailers, for hauling junk, branches or yard waste in the fall. Jackpot! A solid tarp and some rope will turn that into a waterproof "stockpile transport" system.

Here's the deal with expanding the BOLT concept. You have to remain realistic and keep your priorities straight. Don't mix and match two fifty-gallon bins if you can't fit both of them in one car. Taking two cars might sound like a grand idea while quietly sipping the drink of your choice and formulating the "bug out" portion of your personal readiness plan. That idea might disintegrate in the driveway when the first distant gunshot reaches your ears. Not a good time to "unscrew" the two bins. Plan for the expanded essentials to fit in one car.

I mentioned gunshots, so a quick word about security is in order. Fumbling around in a dark basement for the hidden key to the gun safe is not the best use of your time in a crisis. Neither is loading magazines, rigging your sweet tacti-cool vest, adjusting your holster…the list goes on. Firearms, if they're part of your immediate or extended "Bug Out" plan, need to be readily accessible and ready to use.

The "readily accessible and ready to use" rule applies to travel as well. Unless you have heavily tinted windows and no external trailers or rooftop carriers, your preparedness will draw attention. The wrong kind of attention. And just in case you're saying, "But I do have heavily tinted windows, and I don't plan to use a trailer," guess what? I can tell when your car is loaded down by looking at the tires. Unless your car is a custom "low rider" design (Honda minivan doesn't count), everyone else can tell too. Just be mindful of the fact that your "state of emergency," may not match law enforcement's perception of the need to carry firearms at the moment.

I promised in the last chapter that we'd talk about the Get Home Bag. But isn't that the opposite of the BOLT kit? Kinda. Sorta. Maybe. I like to think of the Get Home Bag as a Get Somewhere Bag. I know. The last thing you need right now is another BAG or KIT to confuse matters. I'll make it easy. The GHB is a mini-version of the BOLT kit. We typically mention it as something to keep in your car at all times to facilitate your return home, but I recommend having an additional GHB at home for quick trips outside of the home during a disaster or as added protection during a family vacation (throw it in the car). The Kit concept is meant to be flexible, with some fundamentals. If you embrace the idea of having prepacked kits for multiple purposes, you're well on your way to laying a solid foundation for the rest of your readiness plan.

PART 4: THE BIG(ger) PICTURE

Chapter 17: LET'S GO CAMPING

Alex took several sheets of paper and three maps from a small green backpack he'd carried into the house. "I have a few checklists that each family will need to follow," he said. He handed a sheet of paper to each family, giving theirs to Kate. "The first sheet is for the bicycle group. This is a watered-down bug-out or BOLT kit. The focus is on mobility and balance while riding, so anything not directly related to hydration, nutrition, and short-term survival has been scratched from the list. Under ideal, casual cycling conditions, the trip should take no more than four to five hours. You're looking at thirty-five miles taking the shortest route. Given the circumstances, I think you should plan for the possibility of an overnight. Thirty-six hours at the outside, accounting for detours, roadblocks, hiding out—whatever. I can't imagine any scenario other than capture that would keep you from reaching your destination within that timeframe, and I highly doubt anyone will get close enough to you to do that. Everything on this list will fit into a medium-sized rucksack with room to spare."

"No sleeping bags?" said Samantha. "We don't have Gore-Tex shells."

"If you have some highly compressible bags, that should be fine. I was just trying to keep the weight to a minimum. Water, MREs, first aid and tents are the highest priority," said Alex.

—From *The Perseid Collapse*

Steven

You will either love us or hate us for including this chapter. I say this because nobody reacts the same to the great outdoors experience. Some embrace every moment of it. Others can take it or leave it. The rest? They're the reason I highly advise you to introduce your survival team to camping. I don't say this because I want the nation's divorce rate to skyrocket. Campcraft, as I'll sometimes call it from this point forward, is a fundamental skill that can make the difference between a *self-sustaining* readiness plan and a *self-limiting* one.

Before we begin, let me clarify my concept of campcraft, since everyone has a different definition. For those of you familiar with campgrounds, you know what I'm talking about. There's the young couple with a small tent, sitting on the ground by their fire pit...right next to the slickest camping setup you've ever seen. Ten-person tent with screened-in sitting area, portable wash basin with faucet (somehow spouting water—I've seen this), two propane grills, air mattresses inside the tent (you heard the air compressor earlier), nine coolers, AstroTurf carpeting covering up that nasty dirt (seen this too)...and many more conveniences of the modern world. *For our purposes, this is not camping.*

I'm not saying you have to "go native," but at the very least you should start with the gear included in your basic and expanded BOLT kits. Did you catch what I did there? I just gave you a practical reason to assemble a BOLT kit and a tactical reason to use it. *Practical* because this is one of the few categories discussed where the gear can simultaneously serve a dual purpose. Recreation and readiness. *Tactical* because camping is a way to physically rehearse an important part of your personal readiness plan. Even with fancy equipment and a positive attitude, camping always presents challenges that will hone your basic campcraft skills. It's the ultimate learning laboratory—with few rules besides "respect your fellow camper."

What can you learn in a relatively sterile, campground environment? The list is extensive:

-How to set up your tent in the dark. You'll arrive late at some point in your camping career.
-How to set up your tent in the day. Had to include that one.
-Where to set up your tent? Dry ground, shaded, sheltered from the wind, not under a large, dead branch. I could keep going here, even for a regulated site.
-How to make fire. Not as easy as it sounds. Not talking flint and steel either.
-Tying knots and using rope. We always tie a few tarps over the tent and eating areas.
-Outdoor hygiene. Nothing feels better after three days of camping than brushing your teeth and washing your face. Also, you'll quickly learn how to keep dirt out of your sleeping bag.
-Water conservation (drinking and washing). You'll have access to water, but we find that nobody wants to walk two campsites over to fetch any. Filling a few pots of water for dinner stretches all night.
-Small tool use. There's always something to do around the campsite.
-Plant identification. Poison ivy anyone?
-How to store food. If the park has bears, you'll learn how to store your food to avoid losing it. Most parks will provide directions. None of the directions recommend keeping food in your tent. Most of you at one point or another will see evidence of small creatures in your site—usually raccoons sniffing out a dropped marshmallow.

You'll be a regular Grizzly Adams after the first season! Not really, but you'll learn far more about campcraft than I listed. You'll also learn something about yourself and everyone in your immediate survival team. Camping in a controlled setting is a low-intensity form of adversity. Adversity, in any form, surfaces our strengths and weaknesses. Take mental notes and adjust. If your son can't carry a backpack for more than two hundred feet without throwing a complete fit, time to make some changes to the readiness plan. Little observations and modifications like these can make a big difference when a disaster situation demands performance.

If you can convince your crew to do some backcountry camping, and they've graduated beyond the private campground with a Jacuzzi and pool, I highly suggest it. *"Hiking in"* with the gear on your back is the closest you'll come to a true BOLT experience. I guarantee (the lawyers hate when I say that) you won't regret the experience, if you plan for it properly and stay safe. Watch the weather and don't get lost (easier said than done—another chance to learn).

Speaking of getting lost. Does everyone know how to use a map and a compass? You better hope there's a Boy Scout, Girl Scout, marine, soldier or park ranger in your group. I know, GPS is more accurate, and it's fair to assume that the system will remain online. From my research, it would take one hell of a catastrophe to knock the GPS system out of service—but we like the RULE OF THREES.

There's no easy way to learn land navigation other than practical application. If you do some backcountry camping, you need to have a surveyed map of the area and a compass. In most cases, you'll follow a well-marked trail, but this is a great opportunity to practice basic navigation skills. *Taking azimuths, reading contours, triangulation, adjusting for magnetic deviation, pace count.* If none of these phrases mean anything to you, I recommend finding a basic book about land navigation for your readiness library.

What's the third navigation method? Ask someone in a convenience store. Just kidding. Road maps will come in handy, even on foot. You can follow a road at a safe distance, using it occasionally to navigate natural obstacles (rivers, hills). We keep foldable maps of the entire New England region in our BOLT kits.

I just got "lost" myself talking about land navigation, so I'll finish this topic where I started. I mentioned that campcraft can spell the difference between a **self-sustaining** readiness plan and a **self-limiting** one. Campcraft has no boundaries (except those set by state and federal laws). If fully embraced, you can learn nearly every skill necessary to survive on the land. Fishing, hunting (snares and basic traps), foraging for edible plants and bugs, preserving food, water procurement and sterilization, shelter building (with natural materials or far more basic supplies), navigation, concealment, fire building—ALL WHILE RECREATING! Technically.

Want to know a secret? You can learn most of these skills in your backyard. Don't start snaring squirrels in your neighborhood! That will lead to police calls and funny looks from your neighbors. They already think you're crazy because the UPS truck pulls up twice a day to deliver your readiness supplies. Seriously, the "backyard camp out" is the most overlooked campcraft resource available to many of us (sorry, urban warriors). You can build a shelter between two trees with string and a tarp, with the full comfort of knowing that you can walk fifty feet and step into an air-conditioned house if something goes awry.

I'll end this with a bonus campcraft recipe! Forest Lemonade. I learned this in SERE (Survival Escape Resistance Evasion) school.

1. Find an ample supply of black ants (preferably the big ones).

2. Pinch the heads off about fifteen to twenty ants and mash them in a cup. Have I lost anyone yet? Make sure to pinch all of the heads, or you might get a pinch on the inside of your mouth. Not making any of this up.

3. Add sterilized water to the cup and taste. Add more ants to increase bitterness. Add more water to decrease.

4. Enjoy the health benefits of eating ants. The Chinese have been eating ants for millennia to treat diseases like rheumatism. They also provide protein.

Who wants another recipe? Hello?

Randall

Ah yes, the great outdoors. Some people love it, others not so much, and some have absolutely no idea what I'm talking about. Thankfully I'm not in that last group, but believe it or not, I know more than a few that are. Remember those cool parents of mine that I told you about in the last chapter? Well, thanks to their efforts and the simple blessing of growing up rural, I am no stranger to the beauty and wonder that spending time outside has to offer.

Some of my favorite memories of growing up take me right back to a sunrise campfire by the lake with my dad, my mom and my brother. We would cook our meals right over the fire and "rough it" for a few days without a shower. By the end of the week we were all tired and ready to get back home, but those memories are the gems that I carry with me to this day. Good stuff.

You may have thought that all sounded like a lot of fun, maybe even a bit charming, but take a closer look at what was really going on. There was a lot of teaching and learning happening back in those days by the lake, even if I didn't know it at the time. Let's break it down.

Take that sunrise campfire. Sunrise means that we must've been out in the woods overnight, and that means we had to sleep somewhere. That somewhere would be in a tent. Okay, but that means we had to know how and where to set that tent up, right? Yep. And that wonderful fire burning beautiful and low as a father sits with his sons and takes in a majestic morning by the water? Well, somebody had to build it, right? That's right. Good thing they did, too, because we eventually had to eat, and that water for the oatmeal wasn't going to boil itself. And showers, who needs them? If you're a kid running around in the summer woods for a couple of days, showers are *way* down on your priority list behind things like skipping stones and chasing lightning bugs. Besides, a quick dip in the lake will wash all that dirt off just fine, right? Sure, but putting the obvious points on proper hygiene aside for the moment since our parents always made sure that part actually happened, the bigger point here is it is surprising how quickly your priorities change when you're focused on things like shelter, fire, food, water and (more importantly for a young child camping with his family) FUN!

Did you see what was going on there? With an activity as simple as a family camping trip, my parents were teaching us basic survival skills by the bushel and giving us memories to cherish for a lifetime in the process. I know I may be biased, but that's how it's done, folks. Even a one-night adventure in the "great outdoors" near where you live can teach you more about basic campcraft and survival skills than you may have ever thought possible, not to mention all that it will inevitably teach you about yourself and others in your family or group. This is a prime example of the Practical Tactical Preparedness Cycle in action. Camping gets you out in the field and puts your skills and gear to the test...and it's fun too.

Chapter 18: HARDWARE VS. SOFTWARE

"You want me to start firing?" said Cole.

"**** yeah!" he said.

"Does this thing have a safety?"

"I didn't see one," said Bertelson, examining the metal along the right side of the machine gun. "Didn't you train on this gun?"

Bertelson knew how to load the ammunition belt through the tray, remembering the trick with the extractor. You had to manually lock the extractor forward before closing the feed tray cover. Beyond that, he'd never fired it, which was why he swapped out with Randy. Rank had its privileges.

"I fired it once at a demo, but it was already loaded."

"Pull the bolt back and light these ****ers up already."

Randy Cole yanked the charging handle back and slammed it forward, sighting in for a few seconds. He pulled the trigger and nothing happened. "Are you sure this thing doesn't have a safety?"

"What's the hold up, Liberty Two?" he heard through his earpiece.

Cole examined the left side of the gun and the area under the trigger.

"Pull the charging handle back again," Bertelson said. "Maybe it didn't chamber right."

"Liberty Two, this is Actual. What the **** is the hold up?"

Bertelson leaned on his side to access the radio attached to the front of his chest rig. A wet crack stopped him from pressing the transmit button.

What the hell?

The raspberry bush above the gun barrel snapped and fell on the metal cylinder, immediately followed by a sickening wet splash. He twisted on his back to face Cole.

"Pull the damn—"

The gunner's head rested against the machine gun's stock, still facing down the weapon's sights. Eyes wide open, he looked fine except for the two small holes punched through his forehead. A bright crimson mist settled over Cole's gore-covered legs. Bertelson felt a deep, driving pain in his upper back, paralyzing him in place as gunfire erupted. He never felt the rounds that ended his life.

—From *Event Horizon*

Randall

I love gear. Love it. Whether we're talking about the slickest looking new fan gear in the colors of my favorite college sports team (*How 'bout them DAWGS!*), a new "old" guitar or a new piece of battle-rattle kit, I love gear. Gear is the stuff or the **hardware** that goes along with any interest.

The saving grace in my situation is that I know I have a weakness for this **hardware** and I embrace it. I don't run from this fact because I believe in all of the advantages a strong kit provides. When it comes to the things that really matter, I do not hesitate to get the highest quality gear I can afford that meets the needs of my preparedness plan, but here comes the cold water bath of truth. Quality gear in your kit certainly increases your chances of success, but it does not guarantee it.

High-quality equipment gives you an obvious tactical advantage in any situation, but it can all be undone if you have no idea how to use that equipment properly. You have to develop the skills to maximize its potential through practice and training. ***Software***. That new guitar may look great, but if you don't know where the notes and chords are along the fret board, you might as well be playing *Guitar Hero*. You might have a brand-new rifle and the best night vision gear money can buy, but if you don't get the proper training to go with that gear, you'll be stumbling around in the dark and be about as tactical as a circus clown. *Wait, I think I've heard that somewhere before*. Anyway, the point is all of your fancy gear is pointless (and possibly dangerous) if you don't know how to use it. Practice and training are the ***software*** that makes your ***hardware*** something more than just an expensive ornament.

How do you identify the gear that really matters or how much money you should spend on it? What about sorting out whether it actually fits your plan? Think back to our chapter on "Framing the Basics" for a moment and recall what makes up the Preparedness Prism: planning, purpose of use and practice. Regardless of the type of gear we're talking about, the light of clarity shining through the Prism will burn away the fog of confusion cloaking your planning and performance and raise your game. Just trust what it shows you.

Using the Prism to guide my choices, I have great peace of mind knowing I have what I really need, why I have it, and I've taken the follow-up step of educating myself or getting the training necessary to make sure I know how to use it. I have discovered that having the gear I chose, that I'm proud to own, and most importantly that I can absolutely trust provides a psychological boost that cannot be quantified. This idea fits right in with the survivor mindset and mental toughness, but it also provides the added bonus of raising your confidence level.

My brother and I played sports growing up, and like my dad always said, "If you look good, you feel good, and if you feel good, you play good." Now, how we looked had no direct impact on the outcome of the game. Clearly, the result we earned was based on the game plan, how well we had practiced and our skill level, but there was a gem buried in that message. In preparedness, as in athletics, you want to give yourself every advantage possible in all situations. That's kind of the point. *Survival mindset.* How well you (or your disaster plan) perform in an emergency will be determined by the level of thought put into your planning, how often you practice your plan, and the focus and intensity of your training. With that said, feeling good about yourself builds confidence, and that confidence in yourself and your skills could be the X-factor that keeps you going when things get tough. *Mental toughness.* The better place you're in psychologically, the greater the chances you will perform at a higher level when the time comes.

It's always exciting to get some new preparedness "widget" to add to my *hardware*, but I get just as excited about picking up a new book, taking a class or completing a kick-ass training session to upgrade my *software. You haven't seen anything until you've seen a grown man dance around the kitchen with a huge grin on his face as he listens to the lids on his canning jars "pop" as they securely seal into place.* To our way of thinking, this is one concept that cannot be decoupled. One without the other renders the entire endeavor pointless. This concept of the *hardware* and *software* of your preparedness plan working together applies to each of the basic tenets of preparedness and is the glue that holds everything together. So in conclusion, go forth and prosper! Pick up all the cool new *hardware* you need to get the job done when it comes to preparedness, just don't neglect to kit up your plan with the *software* you need to be successful. If you leave out that last part, you may as well go play *Guitar Hero.*

Steven

Gear vs. training. Buying cool gadgets vs. learning how to effectively use the gadget. Relying on equipment vs. relying on skills. Investing money in stuff vs. investing time (and money) in skills. **Versus** is a preposition "used to indicate two different things, choices, etc., that are being compared or considered" according to Merriam-Webster dictionary. In other words "against." Our title is a little misleading, on purpose. If I had wanted to be a little more honest with the chapter title, it should read "The Balance Between Hardware and Software."

I think it's fair to say that we tend to put more emphasis on the hardware side of the equation in just about every other aspect of our lives. Personal readiness planning will be no exception to this observation unless you make a concerted effort to rebalance our natural tendency to buy the gear first and figure out if you can use it later. I'm not talking about buying the Big Kahuna stockpile of dehydrated food that we mentioned several chapters back. We all know how to cut open plastic, boil water and chew. Mission complete.

I'm talking about purchases like the family's shiny black, tricked-out AR15 (*keep calling it the family's—that draws attention away from the Visa bill*). If you've never fired a rifle before or your grand sum of firearms experience is a .22-caliber bolt-action Ruger, you're in for a little surprise. It's not the same as *Call of Duty*! When you put the crosshair on a target, you don't always hit it...especially if you don't know how to properly zero the scope. It takes years of practice to become proficient with any firearm—*software*. That .22-caliber Ruger might be your best bet for several months, until you consistently hit targets at different ranges—*better software.* I'm not saying you can't buy the rifle of your dreams (we're still friends, right?), I'm saying (1) make sure the basics of your SURVIVE WHAT scenario are covered first (food, water, first aid, etc.), and (2) *commit to training with that rifle.*

It's not fair to focus on firearms. The out of balance hardware versus software syndrome can be found everywhere. I see it every time we're out sailing. The yellow and black Sea Tow boats speed around Casco Bay all day, and they aren't delivering ice for "cooler emergencies." People with no experience on the water buy powerboats and continuously run them aground. Frankly, it's hard to blame the boaters, though I do, while swearing up and down like a sailor (because I am one). Unlike automobiles, there is no licensing requirement for boats. No *software* (training) required! Only *hardware* (the equipment)—and who has time to schedule a coastal navigation and safety course, let alone show up? Red buoy? Green buoy? The water looks clear to me! Crunch. I can make these jokes, because I spent years in the navy, studying marine navigation in all of its agonizing forms. When we bought a sailboat, safe navigation was the ONE area in the entire nautical venture where the *software* exceeded the *hardware*—which entitled me to buy a handheld, chart-plotting GPS. I couldn't let the software win!

I like hardware so much, that I'm constantly on the lookout for new gear or ways to improve the gear I already own. As a matter of fact, I have a nice 3X Burris prism sight mounted to one of my rifles. It's been "attached" for three months and hasn't left the house. If the zombies began stumbling into the neighborhood tomorrow, guess who's going to be scrambling to find a screwdriver to detach that scope so he can use the iron sights? Sort of a trick question. I have forty-five-degree angle iron sights mounted to the rifle in case the scope is damaged. My point is still intact. I have some nice hardware, which hasn't been uploaded with the software. Not very useful in an emergency. I did have the experience to know that I needed backup sights. How many AR owners have thought about backing up their scopes with angled sights? It's a small detail, and I'm back to rifles again. How did that happen?

It happened because we tend to put a lot of effort and money into the equipment, thinking we're done. Call it overconfidence. Call it complacency. Call it laziness. Call it whatever you want, but in the end—CALL YOURSELF ON IT! The gear in your basement can't collect dust. You need to train with it. *After a disaster strikes* is not the time to figure out how to purify water with your Katadyn filter. It's certainly not the time to install batteries in your radio scanner and open the instruction booklet. You should have, at a minimum, a basic *hands-on working knowledge* of every piece of gear in your personal readiness stockpile.

You haven't heard me say don't buy the gear first, right? It sounds like I'm implying that, but I'm not. Ready for a curveball? *Sometimes the hardware can be the catalyst for acquiring the software.* You just need to have a plan to put the two in balance. Firearms are a great example of this. I know several people (some relatively naïve to personal firearms ownership), who have bought advanced firearms over the past year and followed through with formal training.

Campcraft is an even better example. The entire campcraft chapter was a classic example of balancing hardware and software. You can't go camping without the gear, and your experience will be marginal at best until you figure out how to use it. The better you get at the software side of campcraft, the less gear you need or want. I might argue that in the case of campcraft, you should strive to tip the scale as far on the side of software as possible.

Software is about recognizing your current limitations (with hardware or a task) and shrinking those limitations through training and practice. Sometimes, a good piece of hardware can make all of the difference to that practice. It's all about balance.

Chapter 19: PRACTICAL CAPITAL

The last shelving unit on this wall, immediately to the left of the hot water tank, held fifteen small, green Coleman propane cans, four rechargeable/battery-operated walkie-talkies, assorted lighters, thirty unscented pillar candles, one hand-crank powered weather/emergency radio, a Uniden handheld scanner, and at least fifty packages of batteries. Staring at the batteries, Alex calculated that the batteries alone were probably worth more than five hundred dollars.

—From *The Jakarta Pandemic*

Steven

You will spend money putting together a personal readiness plan. That's a hell of a way to start a chapter, Steve! Sorry. There's no way around it, and there's no way to sugarcoat it. Unless you're amazingly crafty and already live off the grid in a remote location, you'll have to loosen your death grip on that wallet or purse—to some degree. Fortunately, you won't find any professional guidance specifying a minimum or maximum amount to spend per year, or a specific percentage that needs to be diverted out of your salary like a 401K plan. The amount you spend depends on how much you can afford and are willing to spend. Whether you decide to spend $10 or $10,000, I recommend one guiding principle to help you navigate the daunting world of "readiness finances." ***Make the most practical investments toward your SURVIVE WHAT scenario.*** I could honestly stop right here, but I won't. This is too important to leave in your hands this soon.

Your personal readiness plan is like an insurance policy. You want it to be current and ready to pay out when a disaster threatens your safety. That could be tomorrow. I didn't just give you permission to "break the bank" and buy everything you need to be ready for the next SURVIVE WHAT scenario. What I want you to do is prioritize the most important items on that list, and consider making an investment in your plan at the level you can afford. By the way, we haven't created a list yet. I use the word "list" as a general term for the steps you need to take to prepare yourself for your SURVIVE WHAT scenario. The steps may not involve purchasing equipment. One could be a "take a CPR course taught by your local Red Cross." How do you prioritize this list?

I prioritize items based on two parameters: (1) importance to basic survival and (2) multipurpose use. I'll spend money on a hand-operated portable water purifier before a camping stove, because I can eat cold food and drink cold water in an emergency (satisfies the basic needs of water and food), plus I can take this with me on the road (multiuse). Can you accomplish the same thing with a camp stove? Yes, but a camp stove requires fuel, an ignition source, a suitable location for fire and time to boil water— which then has to be cooled and put into containers. A hand-pumped filter can provide two liters per minute (without any fuss) and satisfy your requirement for water. Are the prices the same? NO! You can get a portable camp stove for $30–40 and individual propane tanks for $4. A hand-pumped water filter will cost $60–70 with replacement cartridges running $15. If you have $40 to spend, you're probably looking at the camp stove for now. I purposely picked this example because it's a tough one.

Depending on your budget, you'll have to make tough calls like that up and down your list. This is why I keep stressing the SURVIVE WHAT scenario. If you jump online right now and form a "survival" list based on the thousands of prepper/survival blog posts and articles available in the public Internet domain, you'd end up with an unmanageable catalog of things you probably don't need. **Kit to Fit.** Remember that from Chapter 4? Decide what you want to accomplish first, and then build your list around that goal. I guarantee it will be a far more manageable and affordable process.

I'm not saying the lists found online and in books aren't helpful. Far from it. Every one of those lists is backed by a person who did considerable research and has used the items in their personal kits. You can learn a lot from these lists, but you can also become seriously overwhelmed—and slightly depressed. We all experience the depression of seeing a comprehensive list and saying, "I don't have enough stuff!" IT'S TRUE! You do not have everything you need to survive a "grid down," Chinese paratrooper invasion of your city. Neither does 99 percent of the "prepper" population—because it's not a likely scenario. Let's focus on the hurricane or ice storm that is guaranteed to hit your county in the next two years.

Hopefully, I've scaled down your list and made it possible for you to invest a little "Practical Capital" in your plan. Before you start cheering too loudly, we should have a quick discussion about quality—and it's obvious ramifications. Bad news first. Investing in quality equipment reduces your buying power. Expensive doesn't mean better quality, but better quality almost always means more expensive. It's one of those universal laws, like "what goes up, must come down" or "no good deed goes unpunished."

The good news? Quality often translates into durability and reliability: two important factors I consider when choosing important gear. Isn't that still bad news for my wallet? Not if you apply the following filter to your purchase habits. Reserve your quality upgrades (if you can afford them) for the most important items in your different kits. Here's a little hint. I've found that quality makes the biggest difference in smaller items, like a compass or a folding knife—and quality doesn't mean saving up for the serrated tactical knife with stainless steel blade and matte-black Tungsten DLC (Diamond-Like Carbon) coating. It means researching quality brands and picking something reasonable (with good reviews) from their catalogue.

The same filter applies to training. I would love to take a string of tactical rifle classes at the SIG SAUER Academy (two hours away) to upload some new tactical *software*, but that money (and time) would be far better spent on backcountry camping gear and a weekend backpacking trip with the family in the White Mountains of New Hampshire. I won't comment on which one I think might be more fun. The camping trip of course!

Randall

By a quick show of hands, who has absolutely no idea what I mean when I say practical capital? Don't worry, neither did I at first because I didn't fully understand the definition of capital. I had always thought of it strictly as an economic term and just hadn't put together how that fit with preparedness. So, I put the Preparedness Prism and the Cycle into action and figured some stuff out.

According to Dictionary.com, capital is "the accumulated wealth, whether in money or property, owned or employed in business by an individual, corporation, etc. capable of being employed in the production of more wealth." Okay, but what is wealth? *To the interwebs!* "Wealth is anything that has utility and is capable of being appropriated or exchanged." *Thanks Dictionary.com!*

Okay, now we know what the dictionary says capital and wealth are, but what do those terms mean to me with regards to preparedness? Think of it like this. You are the individual and your business is preparedness, so your capital is the stuff that gives you the ability to build, make or otherwise create anything that contributes to the benefit of your personal situation or that you can offer in exchange for anything else you may need. Are you still with me? Hang in there, we're getting close.

Now that the nuts and bolts are secure on this ship of preparedness prosperity, we can really get into what constitutes practical capital. Think back to Steve's essay on planning back in chapter four where he flipped the **Kit to Fit** concept on its ear to make a point. The concept of practical capital is the philosophical antithesis of Steve's potential marauders' *Fit the Kit* idea, and it lies at the heart of our holistic approach to preparedness and it's what Practical Tactical is all about. We believe in the idea that if you are applying any of your available resources, whether it's your time, money, tools, knowledge or skills, you're not simply spending capital if you are making an investment in something that will provide for you later or give you some other tangible return on said investment. In the business of preparedness, this can be considered your capital expenditure (CAPEX).

As we've already discussed, we all have to make choices about everything from the type of gear we need to how much we're willing to spend to get it when it comes to kitting out our preparedness plans, so how do you make these decisions? Once again, I will refer you to the Preparedness Prism and the Cycle. Use these tools, which are probably approaching razor sharp for you at this point, to determine what gives you the most "bang" for your preparedness buck both in upfront costs and purpose of use and go from there.

Here are a few things to consider regarding practical capital as you evaluate your holdings and what may be valuable to you going forward. Your wealth exists in many forms beyond financial, including social, natural, *"hard"* and intellectual capital. Let's take a closer look at some things that you should consider forms of capital you may have at your disposal…

Financial Capital: This one's pretty straightforward, consisting of anything that can be used as a medium of exchange, including but not limited to dollar bills. It is helpful to remember that an accumulation of money or paper assets is not actual wealth, but a claim on things that constitute actual wealth like natural resources, productive farmland or useful tools. There is no need to spend a lot of time on this, but I did want to point it out.

Social Capital: Like it or not, when it comes to preparedness, it really does take a village, so to speak. When you look at the logistics of a well-rounded preparedness plan, the real world realities tell us the lone wolf survivor is a breed bound for extinction. There is simply too much to do to effectively execute a successful plan of preparedness by oneself. The thing about social capital is you need to spend it to build it. Including family and friends, you may also want to become better acquainted with your neighbors and co-workers to strengthen your preparedness community. Since you're already well on your way with regards to preparedness, you could offer to share your skills, labor or knowledge to help someone else who is just beginning their preparedness journey. You never know, you may just make a new friend and possibly find a future member of your team along the way. Either way, your community will be stronger as a result.

Natural Capital: Take a moment to look around you. Virtually everything you see could be considered natural capital. Everything from the air you breathe and the food you eat to the trees growing in your back yard is natural capital. It gives and sustains life. How you choose to deploy these real assets is up to you, just do not overlook them.

"Hard" Capital: In the last chapter we took a look at the difference between **hardware** and **software.** Good thing too, since those concepts are back again. *"Hard"* capital is the stuff you use to

make other stuff or get things done. Basic handheld tools that you might find in your average backyard shed or shop fit the bill. As Isherwood Williams (Ish) shows us in George R. Stewart's epic, post-apocalyptic novel *Earth Abides*, sometimes you just need a good hammer. When it comes to tools, there's basic and there's primitive. Our suggestion is to acquire the types of tools that best fit your overall preparedness plan. These tools will most often be found in that backyard shed or shop we mentioned a moment ago, but like everything else in the Practical Tactical approach to preparedness, these too can be scaled to accommodate any of your smaller kits. Think duct tape, 550 cord and your trusty multi-tool.

Intellectual Capital: Everything you know how to do, every practical preparedness skill and planning or training technique in your quiver makes up your readily available intellectual capital. Productive skills like basic survival techniques, the ability to grow or find food, medical skills and knowledge, mechanical prowess, team-building and leadership techniques and coping methods all should be identified and counted among your *"soft"* assets. Do not forget to include your other potentially available assets like the books and videos already in your preparedness library and your access to open resources like public libraries and the Internet, which can be used to continue to grow your intellectual capital.

Here's a piece of advice, don't make the mistake of undervaluing what you have to offer and thereby restricting your buying power in the preparedness marketplace. There are no two ways about it, practicing a preparedness lifestyle or even taking steps to cover the basics of preparedness requires you to spend some of your hard-earned capital. Hopefully now that you have a real handle on what we consider practical capital to be and a better idea of the actual wealth you may already possess, you will be well equipped to make solid investments in your preparedness going forward rather than just spending your money on stuff.

Now that you are well armed and ready to go, here's a list of some things (in no particular order) that we think might be good to have on hand for everyday use in general, but especially so in any disaster or survival situation. This is by no means a fully comprehensive list, and I have not tried to make it one, but one that hits most of the high points that will serve as a nice jumping-off point.

TRAINING
Water filters/purifiers
Generators
Portable toilets
Five-gallon plastic buckets
Seasoned firewood (six to twelve months to become dried)
Lamp oil, wicks, lamps (CLEAR)
Moleskin
Coleman fuels
Guns and ammunition
Cleaning kits (for weapons)
Pepper spray
Knives (fighting, hunting, utility)
Machete (quality)
Slingshots and ammunition
Hand can openers
Hand egg beaters
Whisks
Potato masher
Honey/syrups
White, brown sugar
Rice
Dry beans
Wheat (hard red)
Vegetable oil (for cooking)

Charcoal and lighter fluid

Water containers (food grade if for drinking)

Mini heater head (propane—without this item, propane won't heat a room)

Grain grinder (non-electric)

Large propane cylinders (grill cooking, other)

Hard copy resources: build a survival library for reference (woodcraft, gardening techniques, first aid instruction, food procurement)

Hard copy resources: build an entertainment library (to read for enjoyment)

Mantles: Aladdin, Coleman, etc.

Baby supplies: diapers/formula/ointments/aspirin, etc.

Condoms

Washboards

Camping stoves (propane, Coleman and kerosene)

Vitamins

Bar soap (body/washing)

Petroleum jelly

Propane cylinder handle-holder

Feminine hygiene/haircare/skin products

Thermal underwear (tops and bottoms)

Bow saws, axes and hatchets, wedges (honing oil)

Basic construction tools….hammers, screwdrivers

Aluminum foil, regular and heavy duty (great cooking and barter item)

Gasoline containers (plastic)

Garbage bags – various sizes (impossible to have too many)

Toilet paper (you can never have enough)

Medicated body powder

Kleenex

Paper towels

Milk – powdered and condensed

Heirloom garden seeds (non-hybrid)

Clothespins/line/hangers
Coleman's Pump Repair Kit
Tuna fish (in water)
Fire extinguishers (alt: large box of baking soda in every room)
First aid kits
Batteries (standardize gear whenever possible, but obtain all sizes…buy furthest-out for expiration dates)
Garlic
Spices
Vinegar
Baking supplies (pans)
Dogs
Dog food
Flour
Yeast
Salt
Matches (wooden)
Writing paper/pads/pencils
Solar calculators
Insulated ice chests
Work boots
Belts
Durable pants and shirts
Flashlights
Headlamp
Light sticks
Lanterns (globes)
Fishing gear: poles, reels, line, hooks, floats, nets, etc.
Journals, diaries and scrapbooks (jot down ideas, feelings, experience; historic times)
Garbage cans – plastic
Men's hygiene: shampoo, toothbrush/paste, mouthwash/floss, nail clippers, etc.
Cast iron cookware (sturdy, efficient)

Fishing supplies/tools
Mosquito coils/repellent, sprays/creams
Duct tape
Tarps/stakes/twine/rope/spikes
Plastic sheeting
Candles
Laundry detergent (liquid)
Backpacks, duffel bags
Garden tools & supplies
Scissors, fabrics & sewing supplies
Canned fruits
Canned veggies
Canned soups, stews, etc.
Bleach (plain, NOT scented)
Canning supplies (jars/lids/wax)
Knives and sharpening tools: files, stones, steel
Bicycles: tires/tubes/pumps/chains, etc
Sleeping bags and blankets/pillows/mats
Carbon monoxide alarm (battery powered)
Board games, cards, dice
Rat poisons and roach killer
Mousetraps, ant traps & cockroach magnets
Paper plates/cups/utensils (stock up, folks)
Baby wipes, oils, waterless & antibacterial soap (saves a lot of water)
Rain gear, rubberized boots, etc.
Shaving supplies (razors & creams, talc, after shave)
Hand pumps & siphons (for water and for fuels)
Soy sauce
Bullion/gravy/soup bases
Reading glasses
Chocolate/cocoa/Tang/punch (water enhancers)
Woolen clothing, scarves/earmuffs/mittens
Boy Scout Handbook

Roll-on window insulation kit
Graham crackers, saltines, pretzels
Trail mix/jerky
Popcorn, peanut butter, nuts
Socks
Underwear, T-shirts, etc.
Lumber (all types and sizes)
Wagons and carts
Cots and inflatable mattresses
Gloves: work/warming/gardening, etc.
Lantern hangers
Screen patches
Barometer/temperature/humidity gauge (analog)
Glue
Nails
Screws
Nuts and bolts
Teas
Coffee
Cigarettes
Wine/liquors (barter, medicinal, etc.)
Paraffin wax
Chewing gum/candies
Atomizers (for cooling/bathing)
Hats
Safety glasses
Large zip ties
Head dressing/scarves/wraps
Goats/chickens/rabbits
Motor oil
WD-40
All purpose grease
Chainsaw (chains/sharpeners)
2-cycle oil

Chapter 20 HOMESTEADING

His parents lived on an isolated farm near Limerick, Maine, thirty-two miles west of Scarborough. Alex had purchased a large parcel of lakefront property and built a custom-designed, sustainable home for them, with the idea that the farm would serve as the Fletcher family stronghold if another disaster or pandemic ever hit Maine. Alex and his clan spent at least two days a week at the farm in the summer, helping with the massive garden, which required constant attention. Over the course of five years, the two families had turned the twenty-acre parcel of land into a self-sustainable family compound.

—From *The Perseid Collapse*

"Charlie has a good plot of land next to a pristine lake. I packed up a kit with enough seeds for two seasons and a slightly worn copy of a book we've used to figure out a lot of this homesteading stuff. Sort of a dummies guide to self-sustainability."

"I can't take the book from you," said Ed.

"If we stay here, I'll borrow it back from you in the spring. If not, the book is better off in your hands. I don't think we'll have much need for it where we're headed."

—From *Point of Crisis*

Steven

See Randy's essay. The End. Oh, I have to talk about this subject? Good heavens, I tore out my garden after Randy told me it takes an acre of planting to feed the average person for an entire year.

What's the point, right? As you well know, I didn't tear out my garden—nor did I rush out and dig up the rest of my yard to plant a massive wheat field. ***The concept of homesteading isn't an all-or-nothing venture.*** For most of us, the term homesteading represents a step in the right direction. Rome wasn't built in a day.

First, let's turn to Wikipedia for a definition of homesteading. *"Broadly defined, homesteading is a lifestyle of self-sufficiency. It is characterized by subsistence agriculture, home preservation of foodstuffs, and it may or may not also involve small scale production of textiles, clothing and craftwork for household use or sale."* See, I told you! Homesteading sounds like a lot of work to me, as in sunrise-to-sunset work. I'm not ashamed to admit that I'm not ready for this, and I suspect you aren't ready to embrace the Amish lifestyle either.

So, where do we go from here? Baby steps in the direction of self-sufficiency. Some of us are capable of running a homesteading marathon, others a self-sufficiency 10K and the rest—a few potted tomato plants on your apartment balcony. It all counts, because homesteading on any scale is about developing the ***software*** to build self-sufficiency skills. There's no end! It's a continuum of adaptation and learning. Something is better than nothing, and I'm not saying this to make you feel better.

Four summers ago, we bought all of our food from the grocery stores, markets (in the summer) and a farm share. Today, we still buy most of our food from grocery stores, but we stopped visiting markets and participating in the farm share because our backyard garden provides a nearly endless supply of summer vegetables. Lettuce, carrots, bush beans, pole beans, kale, beets, onions, garlic, arugula, zucchini, tomatoes, cucumbers, celery, strawberries and herbs. By late July, we have to make a concerted effort to harvest the food.

Of course, the garden hasn't been all fun and games for us. Last year, our tomato harvest was horrible, and bore worms attacked and destroyed nearly all of our squash. We didn't plant squash this year. We've dealt with several types of pests over the past three years, each time learning a little more about how to handle garden pestilence—a useful skill if you depend on the food to survive. Beyond fighting worms, spores and bugs, we've learned how to compost, rotate plantings each season to nourish depleted soil and how to thin different plants for maximum food production. This year I'm growing a small crop of dry beans for winter storage (protein source), and we'll try to recapture seeds from heirloom vegetables. Every season, we upgrade our homesteading *software*, which brings us a little further down the self-sufficiency path.

I mentioned farm shares, which is a great way for "urban homesteaders" or "city slickers" to indirectly participate in homesteading. You basically pay a monthly fee to have fresh vegetables and farm products delivered to the city for pickup on a certain day at a specified location. Most of the farms hold events on their property and encourage members to volunteer time. If you want to take the concept a step further, you can seek out a community garden. A community garden is a public plot of land that is divided into small parcels, where each person or group is responsible for their own gardening. Most major cities offer community gardening—New York City boasts 600 gardens spread across the five boroughs.

I'm going to leave you with a little homework. Trust me, it'll be fun. You absolutely have to watch a PBS show called *Frontier House*. You can find all of the episodes on YouTube. The show takes three modern families and transports them back in time to the "land rush" days in Montana. They arrive in the late spring and have until the end of the summer to create a self-sufficient homestead that can survive an eight-month Montana winter. It's an eye-opening look at what it would take to be truly self-sustaining in a long term, grid-down scenario. If you don't plan on checking out the show, I'll give you the quick version. It won't be easy— especially if you haven't taken a few steps down the homesteading path.

Randall

If there were ever a phrase in the preparedness lexicon that needed to be defined as to how it fits into today's modern world, it's homesteading. Just so you know, I've looked at the dictionary's definition, and it feels a little vague to me. So I've decided to share the working definition that we use because it states more clearly the way we view the act of homesteading and explains how we feel it fits into our daily lives. For our purposes, the term homesteading simply refers to a lifestyle that promotes greater self-sufficiency and resilience while providing insurance against "the system" by simplifying the complexities of our modern society and our lives down to focus on addressing our basic needs.

Think back to chapter 8 for a moment. I talked about taking steps to strengthen your food resilience by "creating an edible landscape or adding small stock to your backyard community." For us, this is just one aspect of what the overall philosophy of homesteading is all about. Guided by how we define homesteading, we looked at our situation, taking into account all of our available forms of capital, and developed a system that makes our property work *for* us rather than just being something we have to work to keep.

For instance, everyone has to eat. We asked ourselves, "What can we do to grow more of our own food right here?" From there we set out a plan and went to work. Today, when you look around our backyard, you'll see a good-sized traditional vegetable garden, a mini-orchard with apple and peach trees and even a lemon tree. Beside the mini-orchard you'll find our beautiful chicken coop. We currently have nine hens, and our ladies provide us with an average of six to seven fresh eggs daily. This year we've upgraded our gardening efforts and have built several new raised garden beds spread around the property. *Resilience.* What about water? You can't live without it, so we decided to do what we could to lessen our exposure to a disruption of the municipal water service by building a 750-gallon rain catchment system. We use this harvested resource to water our summer gardens, the mini-orchard and the animals. It is also a primary water source in our family disaster plan. *Resilience.* Of course, there are skills that must be learned along every step of this homesteading road, and we have fully embraced the process. From learning the art of canning so we can preserve the excess food that comes from our vegetable gardens, how to engineer the plumbing that carries water around the property from the rain catchment system, to logging the timber on our property for firewood as we clear space for some new project, there is always some new skill to learn and more work to be done. *Resilience.*

These are just a few examples of what we have done to strengthen our position by building resilience into our daily lives, yet there is so much more that we want to do. We would love to take up beekeeping, and we have even considered adding an aquaponics system to our preparedness infrastructure, so we'll see what comes next.

We have built a system that works *for* us 24 hours a day, 365 days a year, all while adding depth, beauty and richness to our lives in every way. The real magic of the system is that it all works together, one part to the benefit of the next. The hens not only provide us with eggs that we eat, their waste goes into the compost, which enriches the soil that we put back into our garden, which produces food that we eat. The vegetable gardens not only provide us with fresh, organic food, but we also use the excess bounty to make jellies and other foods that we can give as gifts or use as barter goods. The water from the rain catchment system irrigates our gardens and the fruit trees, but it is also a source of water for the hens. And so it goes.

There is simply too much involved with homesteading for me to mention it all here, so I won't even try. I'll just recommend the one resource that we consider indispensable on all matters related to the topic, *The Encyclopedia of Country Living* by Carla Emery. If you have any interest in wandering further down the homesteading road, do yourself a favor and add this gem to your library immediately. Regardless of the level of homesteading activity you choose to include in your plan, just know that it is enough. Any and every step you take in your journey should be considered a success because you will have undoubtedly achieved a goal or learned some new skill, thereby strengthening your preparedness situation, and I'm willing to bet you'll discover you've added a little depth, beauty and richness of your own along the way. I know you can do it. All that's left is to get out there, get dirty and get it done. *Happy Homesteading!*

Chapter 21: VALUE

Randall

Value is not a hard concept to grasp. We all have some basic understanding of what it means to say something has value. It means some thing has worth, that it is worth something. It can't be that deep a subject, right? Well, sort of. We decided to title this chapter VALUE because this word does, in fact, have more than one meaning. Not in the basic definition of the word, but in how the context in which the word is used colors its actual meaning. I'll explain.

In the last chapter I talked about practical capital and actual wealth and offered a few examples of things that are worth a great deal because they give you the ability to increase your productivity going forward. So what does value mean? *Back to the interwebs!* According to Dictionary.com value is "the relative worth, merit or importance" of an object, skill or piece of information. See? Context! "Thing 1" that may not have value in one situation could prove to be extremely valuable in a different situation. It really all depends on what "Thing 1" is and what the situation is when it is being considered.

In our everyday lives, if there is an emergency like a compound fracture to a lower leg, the solution is simple. We immediately head to the nearest emergency room for treatment. But what if the situation were to change? What if you are dealing with the same emergency, but you can't get the injured person to the emergency room because a tornado has just decimated your community, debris is blocking the roadways, and "Oh, by the way…" your vehicle is lodged in the tree down the street? In that moment, if there is someone that knows basic first aid and understands how to treat that injury nearby, their inherent value will skyrocket.

Practical tools and skills already have real-world value, and in a time of emergency or disaster those items will only see their value increase, but what if our disaster situation deepens into a "Konkoly level" event? For instance, the United States dollar has value. Of course it does. I have dollars, and dollars are good. Today. But, what if my situation were to change? In Steve's work, *The Perseid Collapse*, a tsunami ravages the New England area, and the lights go out and don't come back on. As our characters figure this out, things like quality water filters, stored food, a battle rifle and a working vehicle instantly become exponentially more valuable and the relative value of the mighty US dollar, the reserve currency of the entire world, simply melts away. In a matter of hours, we see the system of claims in the United States completely collapse.

In this Konkoly apocalypse, we are thrust into a world where having shelter that is safe and secure and the knowledge of how to successfully grow a garden are immeasurably more valuable than a luxury sports car or the film star that owns it. Those type items and skill sets simply cease to matter in a "next level" disaster situation. Items that give you the ability to "cut things, tie things together and set things on fire" will always be classics, but there will be a need extending all the way out to the resilient life skills like having the ability to teach and train others, or maybe having someone in your circle that is trained as an EMT that can serve as a community "doctor" that will prove vital in a long-term disaster situation.

Often when people think of what might have value after a disaster, they think in terms of what might make a good barter item. It is common for people to determine the value of an object, skill or piece of information that can be traded for other goods by only looking through the economic prism, but based on what we learned in the previous chapter, this is a limited perspective. When you understand that you have other forms of capital like social, natural, **"hard"** and intellectual capital at your disposal, you instantly have more options. Instead of swapping "dollars for dollars" as it were, you can volunteer your time or labor to help out on a project or offer to teach someone a new skill as an absolutely viable form of currency to be exchanged.

"Two is one and one is none." Do you remember that old saying? If so, you may be asking yourself, "Why would anyone be willing to part with anything that they feel might help them survive after a disaster, especially a long-term disaster?" The answer is simple. Two hammers. Consider this. I've got two hammers but no screwdriver, and I need a screw driver to finish an important project, while my neighbor has two screwdrivers and no hammer. In this situation, I might be persuaded to trade one of my hammers for one of my neighbor's screwdrivers. It's a win-win and everybody's happy. As you consider your preparedness plans and take stock of your practical capital, I would encourage you to remember how real value is determined and adjust your plans accordingly.

In the world of preparedness, perpetual growth isn't always a good thing, and bigger doesn't always mean better. The concept of real value can also bring a "value added" bonus to every aspect of your life. Some facets of living a preparedness lifestyle require that you slow down, "live smaller" and pay attention to the little things. By choosing to "live smaller" you may find that you voluntarily scale down your life and that you focus more on self and home improvement, which strengthens personal resilience, and less on keeping up with the neighbors. When you focus in and pay more attention to what's going on in your own little world, you begin to discover the beauty and richness that was there all along. *That* has real value.

Steve

SELF-DEFENSE REDUX

Surprise! I let Randy run with the VALUE essay, because I came up relatively blank on a subject that he regularly discusses. Instead, I plan to circle back and address an important aspect of self-defense that I omitted in Chapter 11. The ramifications, legal and otherwise. *Ramifications, Steve? The only ramification I need to be worried about is the safety of my family!* I couldn't agree more, imaginary voice that always helps me make a point, but we need to talk about a few important aspects before I turn you loose.

Before I start to muddy the waters, let's get something straight. ***Nothing suspends the right to defend yourself and your family/friends from an immediate and unavoidable danger of death or grave bodily harm. Period.*** Sounds simple enough, until you dig a little deeper. Quick question—yes or no answer. Can you shoot someone who breaks into your house in the middle of the night? Most of you answered, "YES!" I answered, "Hell yes!" A few of you answered, "Just make sure you don't shoot them in the back." I like the way all of you think, especially the last group!

In the forty-six states with defined Castle Doctrine laws, all of you would be correct—if you can establish the elements required to act in self-defense. That's right, even states with Castle Doctrine and Stand Your Ground laws still require the elements of self-defense. Do you know the basic elements?

Ability: The attacker has the power to inflict death or grave bodily harm. You see a guy in a wheelchair enter the front door of your house at two in the morning with a gun—he certainly has the ***ability*** to kill you. I know a paraplegic is an odd choice for a burglar, but bear with me. If you see that same intruder holding a baseball bat, you need to think long and hard about pulling the trigger of your shotgun. Even though most Castle Doctrine laws do not require you to retreat in your own home, you might have a serious problem explaining why you didn't head upstairs (or stay upstairs) and call 911.

Opportunity: The attacker has the prospect of using his or her ability against you. If you're at the top of the stairs, and the guy in the wheelchair is at the bottom of the stairs waving the baseball bat, the basic element of *opportunity* has not been met. If he tosses the bat aside and draws a pistol from his waistband—very different story.

Jeopardy: The attacker's actions or words give you a reasonable belief that he or she intends to inflict death or grave bodily harm. This is the most subjective element, unless the whole encounter is recorded on your smartphone camera, with sound enabled, and you don't delete it. That's evidence by the way, and I did not suggest you tamper with evidence. I'm just saying that this element relies on your perception of events. Wheelchair or not, carrying a weapon into your house sets the *jeopardy* element in motion. I think most of us would agree with this assessment. What they do with the weapon speaks louder than words.

I'm not a lawyer, so I'm going to stop there and let you ponder the finer points of the basic elements. *Keep in mind that the basic elements and your right to self-defense are not restricted to your home.* They apply anywhere you are legally entitled to be. What does that mean? If you're out shopping for Friday night's barbeque fixings, and someone pulls a gun or knife on you in the parking lot, you have a right to defend yourself with the concealed weapon in your purse—*as long as you have a concealed carry permit*. Anyone shaking his or her head? Your instincts are good. You still have a right to defend yourself, regardless of whether you've been issued a permit, but you will likely face criminal and civil charges for the unlawful possession of a firearm.

I know what you're going to say in that imaginary voice. *Steve, I'd rather be judged by twelve than carried by six.* Me too, but it's something to think about, especially if you can somehow avoid the situation or defuse it. Ending up behind bars until the police and the local district attorney sort out your situation might not be the best detour during a disaster.

This has serious implications if you plan to "bug out" with firearms. If you travel by car, keeping your firearms out of sight but easily accessible will likely violate state law if you don't have a concealed weapons permit. Regardless of whether you have a permit, keeping an AR-15 next to your seat in an automobile is a "no go." Every state has specific restrictions for the transport of firearms, and most of them specify that the firearms need to travel in locked containers (or trunks), separate from ammunition. Does that mean you should perch them out of the windows for everyone to see? Not a good idea—at all. You're caught between a rock and a hard place travelling by car. Damned if you do, damned if you don't. Use your best judgment and remember that a vast majority of disaster scenarios will not involve mobs of rioting civilians or the planned ambushes of travellers at strategic intersections. At least not in the early stages.

"Bugging out" on foot or bicycle gets interesting. Many states allow open carry of firearms. In Maine, I can walk through downtown Portland with an AR-15 slung across my tactical vest and a pistol in an exposed thigh holster. I assume I can do the same on my mountain bike. All perfectly legal, and all guaranteed to draw a ton of attention. Remember, you want to avoid drawing attention, especially from law enforcement. Frankly, I don't know what to tell you here. In *The Perseid Collapse*, the groups travelling by bike chose to break down their rifles and stow them in their backpacks until they cleared the built-up areas beyond their town. Then again, in *The Perseid Collapse*, they had witnessed law enforcement officers disarming citizens. Once again, this is a judgment call you'll have to make based on the situation. If your car is useless due to flooding, and the civil situation is stable in your area, marching past a police checkpoint with the same "load-out" as a marine deployed to Afghanistan might not be your best option.

This brings us to the controversy at the heart of *The Jakarta Pandemic.* Steven Konkoly, the author, has been criticized on a number of occasions for Alex Fletcher's "poor firearms handling decisions and failure to defend his family." I'm not going to recap the situations and defend Alex's decisions, because I saddled Alex with difficult situations to make a point. No situation is black and white. A little thought might be required, especially outside of the "castle."

I didn't give Alex a simple home invasion. That would be far too easy. Instead, I put him in a series of escalating encounters, none of which satisfied the basic elements of self-defense and all of which took place outside of his home. Readers wanted Alex to shoot the "bad guys" during the first encounter, and so did I, but Alex saw the bigger picture. The police were still responding to 911 calls, and gunning down three armed men in the middle of the street would have earned him a trip to the police station during the worst pandemic in human history—along with a search of his house and the confiscation of his firearms. Of course, as readers we knew his decision would have deeper consequences within the neighborhood, and that he'd eventually regret not shooting them earlier. *As a writer, I have to blur these lines, because it creates better fiction.* I don't envy anyone faced with a life-and-death self-defense decision. *In the real world, you don't get to rewrite the chapter if you make the wrong decision.*

My best recommendation is that you learn your state laws cold and mentally rehearse scenarios, in and out of the home, that may require you to defend yourself, family member or friend.

Chapter 22: THE HUMAN FACTOR

"The last thing is the most important. I noticed people outside, and it sounds like Charlie has been helping other neighbors to move bodies. We need to minimize contact with the neighbors, and keep our packing efforts a secret. We'll have to move all the gear over to Ed's at night. Our departure tomorrow needs to remain a secret. I can't stress that enough. It sounds cold, but it's our reality. We all have friends in the neighborhood, and for the most part, they should be fine once the basements drain. We did our part after the pandemic. Most of the neighbors have stockpiled food and supplies. I can't run a neighborhood refugee camp out at my parents' farm. It's as simple as that."

Alex didn't sense any problem with his last statement. They all understood the gravity and reality of the situation. Even with a sizable food stockpile and the ability to filter water, life would be extremely difficult in the neighborhood. Most home foundations were more than likely cracked. Some would collapse. The epic scale of this disaster guaranteed that nothing would be restored or repaired for several months, eventually forcing most people to migrate or face a brutal winter with meager supplies and limited essential services. He could envision massive FEMA camps established to handle the overflow of humanity fleeing New England, followed by disease, starvation and depravity. Nobody at the Walkers' kitchen table wanted to stick around for that end game.

—From *The Perseid Collapse*

Steven

Unless you currently live in a fortified, well-stocked silo far beyond the edges of humanity, you'll have to deal with people when a disaster strikes. They're everywhere! Across the street, down the road, in the grocery store, on the roads in cars—every time I turn my head I see more people. The problem isn't going away. Problem? Yes and no. Readiness planning is intrinsically YOU-centric. Let's face it, you're not putting together a plan and expending resources for the neighbors. Handing out BOLT kits to the neighbors would be a friendly gesture when the county sheriff arrives to give your block the one-hour wildfire evacuation notice, but unless you just won the lottery and have inordinate amounts of time on your hands, it's not a practical strategy. *Charity begins at home,* so start there. I'm sure I just misused that quote.

So, when the big pandemic hits or snipers collapse the electrical grid for several months, should you lock your doors, shutter the windows and post a "GO AWAY" sign on your door? The Fletchers tried that in my first novel, *The Jakarta Pandemic,* and it didn't work out so well for them. We don't live in a vacuum, and despite our natural instinct to turn inward at the outset of a crisis, eventually most of us do a one-eighty and reach out to others. Herd mentality. Mob mentality. Safety in numbers. Call it what you will, but people naturally band together in times of adversity— especially when they haven't prepared. Sorry. That's my cynical side slipping through again. Let me start over. ***People tend to gather in groups during a crisis for safety, information and resources.*** You should be proud! I mentioned resources last— begrudgingly.

I took some heat for *The Jakarta Pandemic* from readers who thought the Fletchers were selfish jerks. This group of readers was an infinitesimally small minority, but I learned something important from them. *They're better people than I am, and I'm fine with that!* Seriously, if being a "selfish jerk" means that my family survives a disaster, (without taking active steps to hasten the demise of others), I can sleep soundly at night.

Did you hear that "prepared is the new selfish"? There's a crazy, counter-preparedness movement based on the premise that "preppers" are socially selfish hoarders. I'm not making this up! Despite the fact that there is no shortage of supplies to buy right now, and "preppers" spend their own money, somehow "preppers" are more selfish than the vast majority of people that WON'T take basic steps to prepare. That's actually not a completely fair portrayal. They'll take steps—enough to reach your house.

Now that's a very cynical view of humanity, and I temper that statement with a disclaimer. ***Bumming from you is not their plan for the apocalypse. It's just the inevitable outcome in dire circumstances.*** Imagine it's three weeks into a crippling pandemic disaster, and you ate through the pantry ten days ago. Your kids are hungry, everyone is cranky, and the rainwater you've depended on to keep the family hydrated is running low. For the first time in your entire life, you're praying for rain in the middle of the summer. You wake up one morning and your youngest child is listless with a high fever.

If you knew that one of your neighbors kept a "prepper" stockpile, which might include medications that could save your child—what would you do? You'd politely knock on their door and ask them some questions about their stockpile and the possibility of sharing any medications that might help your child. That's a natural course of action. What if those neighbors said that they didn't have any medications to spare? Would you head home and tell your spouse, "Lesson learned, honey. They prepared and we didn't. Hey, look at the bright side…one less mouth to feed?" That's NOT a natural course of action, and that's certainly not what I'd be saying. That medicine would find its way to my house, because I know what I'm prepared to do for my family.

Let's stop for a moment and reexamine this scenario. Switch back to the prepared family's side of the equation. Would you really say no to a request like that? I'd have to be down to my last "magic pill" to turn one of my neighbors away under those circumstances. In *The Jakarta Pandemic*, Alex Fletcher shared most of the life-saving medications he had collected over the past year with his neighbors. Being prepared doesn't mean you shouldn't help, but it does mean you should take steps to prevent your house from becoming the neighborhood pharmacy and grocery store.

What exactly does that mean? Sadly, there's no template or blueprint for managing neighborly expectations. Ideally, the majority of your neighbors would be prepared on some level. That would mitigate, if not eliminate, the dark elements of the human factor from all but the most drastic scenarios. Vesting people in their own survival before a disaster is the most effective strategy I can recommend, but how do you accomplish this? Do you proselytize? You could always throw a cocktail party or backyard barbeque, only to bring the dreaded flip chart out after everyone has thrown down some chips and a few drinks. Hey, they'll be happy it's not an Amway presentation and listen with rapt attention! Probably not, but you get my point. The more neighbors you can convince to take preparedness seriously without becoming a nuisance, the better your situation will be when disaster strikes. On the flip side, you've just announced that you're a "prepper," and everyone knows where to go for essential supplies when the lights go out.

Face it; you can't convince everyone to do this. I suggest trying to make a few readiness-minded allies among your friends and neighbors. An inner "crew" watching your back, and vice versa, is the next best thing to achieving "neighborhood readiness nirvana." Another disclaimer: you're still friends with the rest of your neighbors, unless you have other reasons not to be friends. I'm not saying that you need to start "unfriending" the "nonbelievers." Quite the contrary. It should be business as usual in your neighborhood, until it's not. You just need to have some semblance of a plan in place for when "it's not."

If playing nice with the neighbors isn't your thing, maybe it's time to consider that silo in Minnesota. Just make sure to forward your mail to a P.O. box, or you might have unexpected guests.

Randall

With seven billion of us currently on this planet, a human presence is pretty much the one constant you will find in any disaster situation, regardless of your location. If you are lost, stranded and in need of assistance or rescue, this fact will give you heart. If the world is on fire and exploding all around you, it may cause you great distress. Either way, the human factor will impact how you come through the situation.

The way we see it, there are a couple of "mega" categories that people will fall into when you are looking at the world from a preparedness point of view, internal or external as they relate to you and your preparedness plan. Someone that is in your family or otherwise in your preparedness group would fall into the internal category. If an individual is not a member of your family or group prior to the emergency, then they would fall into the external category. This does not mean everyone is thrown into an "us versus them" situation as soon as disaster strikes. The nature of any relationship with anyone in the external category following a disaster has yet to be determined. This concept merely represents a starting point, and there is still much work to be done, regardless of which category we're talking about.

Let's take a closer look at the internal category. This is your family or anyone in your preselected group. Your inner circle, if you will. These are the folks you already know and trust. *That's right! So, are we done here?* Not quite. Being a member of a tight-knit group and knowing who has your back is a great thing, but there are pitfalls that should be considered. The people we are most comfortable with are often the ones we most easily take for granted. We must challenge and train ourselves not to give in to complacency and allow this divisive seed to take root in our personal relationships. It seems obvious that a person's value is represented by more than their ability to provide a skill that can be checked off on some preparedness group checklist, but it is when we are faced with a stressful situation and everyone is on edge that even the most steadfast partnerships can become strained. It is imperative that we keep in mind what it is that makes us human to begin with and that we are all afflicted with the human condition, especially in a disaster. It is in the crucible of crisis that the ability to remain a caring, empathetic and understanding human being will shine the brightest and could prove to be the light that will see you and your group through the storm. At the very least, you will bring calm into a chaotic situation. Survival doesn't happen in a vacuum. Even if your emotional self is a steel trap and you have everything under control, everyone around you brings their own set of circumstances to the situation...*plus* their reaction to the disaster...and all of it will impact how things play out. Being aware of the personal situations of others, including their limitations (both emotional and physical), will only strengthen your team along with your place in it.

Now let's take a look at the external category. This would be everyone outside of your family or group prior to the disaster. Just because these people aren't already in your inner circle does not mean they should be automatically relegated to the road and forgotten. Anyone initially in the external category may become a member of your broader community or possibly even your preparedness team, but they must be fully vetted first. Neighbor or stranger? Friend or foe? Teammate or threat? Those are essentially the questions that you must ask yourself about anyone in the external category after a disaster. There are advantages and disadvantages to playing things close to the vest when it comes to preparedness, so how you go about making that determination is up to you.

Until further notice, we are all in this together when it comes to surviving on this big blue marble. Living with each other on a daily basis has proven to be harder than it should be time and again, so predicting how we will react as individuals during any disaster is impossible. However, that doesn't mean it is an impossibility that we can survive a disaster when it strikes without giving in to our darkest primal instincts. Whether in our internal or external circles, we can choose to strive for the ideals of the human condition by embracing the human factor within each of us. If we can trust one another enough to keep the focus on what makes us stronger as rugged individuals or as members of a team or community instead of what makes us weaker at any level, it is hard to imagine any disaster that cannot be overcome.

Chapter 23: SHOULD I STAY OR SHOULD I GO?

Kate followed Alex up the steps and into the cockpit, where a refreshingly cool sea breeze greeted them, evaporating the small beads of sweat that had formed on Alex's forehead in defiance of the chilly, coastal air. Despite his demeanor, he was terrified by the prospect of what might lie ahead for them. If something big had indeed gone wrong, he had little doubt that society would quickly collapse. Confidence in the government's ability to handle a major crisis was at an all-time low.

The 2013 flu pandemic had exposed the nation's essential service infrastructure to a slow burn, which caused a rapid, critical failure across the board, launching the country into chaos. While the northernmost states and the upper Midwest had added freezing temperatures and winter storms to the disaster already unfolding, the warmer regions were hit the hardest. The harsh winter weather dampened and eventually extinguished the widespread rioting, looting and violence that continued unabated in cities like Atlanta, Dallas, and Los Angeles. Even the Mid-Atlantic cities saw their share of the devastating civil unrest that ultimately claimed just as many lives as the H16N1 virus.

Not much had changed on Capitol Hill. The likelihood of another pandemic virus striking in our lifetime was a statistical impossibility claimed the epidemiologists—and they were probably right. Funding for national emergency preparedness remained level and consistent with pre-2013 levels, with few politicians willing to suggest cuts, especially with over twenty-six million deaths attributable to the inadequate pandemic preparedness budget authorized by Congress in the years leading to the Jakarta Pandemic. Of course, with the U.S. economy making slow but steady gains, even fewer politicians were eager to increase disaster preparedness funding or spend money on infrastructure improvement programs. Major natural disasters had been shrugged off for decades, given a flurry of attention for a month and pushed to the sidelines.

Alex and Kate understood that the United States could not weather another nationwide disaster, and had taken the appropriate precautions to ensure the safety of family and friends. They would all converge on the isolated farm in Limerick, Maine, where they could live off the grid indefinitely, until society settled back into a routine.

—From *The Perseid Collapse*

Steven

The question on everyone's mind. We saved this for last, because we wanted to torture you for a few hundred pages. Well, Randy didn't want to torment you this long, but I overruled his concerns for your mental health. I'm conditioning your fragile minds for the apocalypse! And you'll soon thank me, because the decision to "bug in" or "bug out" is one of the most difficult and impactful decisions you'll face along the personal readiness path.

Difficult, because the circumstances surrounding the decision may not be as clear-cut as "a tsunami is coming" or "the sheriff ordered us to evacuate." This will most often be a gut-wrenching, "counterintuitive at the time" judgment call.

Impactful, because you'll need to scale down your entire readiness world to fit into a single automobile—if you're lucky! I don't even need to emphasize the game-changing nature of shrinking that world into a backpack.

Let's start by analyzing the decision-making process, which starts long before the disaster strikes. In most cases, it should start with your first purchase, because like we've discussed previously, the best use of your hard earned PRACTICAL CAPITAL should be dedicated to items that can be used (and carried) in multiple scenarios. This is one of the reasons we emphasize the BOLT kit/concept so heavily as the critical FOUNDATION of personal preparedness. It gives you a full range of options.

While you're slowly and steadily making initial purchases that can fulfill both the "bug out" and "bug in" role, it makes sense to sit down and discuss the "triggers" that will cause you to seriously consider leaving your primary readiness location. Obviously, an immediate and catastrophic threat to the location's structure would send you running. Think brushfire, tsunami, flash flood, hurricane—I'm sure there are more examples. I consider this a preemptive, not a lot of choice in the matter "bug out." Get your $#@! and get out of dodge. It starts to get a little more complicated after that.

The next decision-making level occurs after the damage has been done. You've survived one of the disasters listed above and returned, OR you've endured a more immediate disaster like an earthquake or tornado (not a lot of warning for those). At this point, you need to make an honest assessment about the stability of the structure you call home, the ability to provide for your BASIC SURVIVAL NEEDS (Is most of your long-term stockpile buried under rubble? Can you find safe water nearby?) and the immediate external safety of your group (has civil order collapsed, or do you suspect it will shortly?). If any of those needs can't be met, it might be time to move on to your Bug Out Location (BOL). This decision won't be easy, but it'll pale in comparison to the next scenario.

Three weeks into a catastrophic, grid-down disaster—and civil order has started to deteriorate. Do you stay in your comfortable suburban home on the outskirts of the city, or pack up the cars and head to your brother-in-law's house a few hundred miles away in rural Vermont? My wife's brother must be sweating our arrival at this point. Nothing about this decision will be easy, because if it's done correctly (in a timely manner), you'll drive out of a quaint neighborhood on quiet roads through town, leaving your home of (fill in the blank) years behind for no apparent reason. It's hard enough tearing someone away from a burning house, let alone purposely abandoning the house you've raised your kids or cats in for twenty years. You need to talk about this scenario at length with your survival team and mentally rehearse the parameters that might put Operation RUN FOR THE HILLS into effect.

Now that you've taken the steps to streamline the "should I stay or should I go" decision-making process...it should no longer resemble a four-hour town council meeting to discuss the pros and cons of adding more parking spaces at the community park...you can move on to the fun part. Road trip! Everyone likes a "road trip," even if it means speeding out of town ahead of the first wave of Chinese paratroopers.

Of course, the "road trip" makes bugging out sound like it has to be some three-day, no-sleep travel marathon. That might not be the case. If your parents, siblings or good friends live across town or several miles away, your first "bug out" option doesn't have to be the Amish community in eastern Pennsylvania, where you plan to forsake your old ways and adopt even older ways. Randy talks about "concentric levels bug out." When Randy talks, I listen.

"Concentric levels of bug out" is a clever phrase for having different bug-out locations at different distances from your home— sort of a modification of the RULE OF THREES. I'm not going to tell you exactly where you should go, or who you should stay with. That's up to you to decide, based on a few guidelines.

Your first location should be a relative or friend (more than one option is advisable) on the other side of town or a few miles away. Not every disaster or SURVIVE WHAT scenario requires a long- or medium-distance bug out. If your home burns down or is destroyed by a tornado, having an immediate, nearby option will ease recovery efforts and allow you to protect what remains of your property. Make sure they know you'll be coming in the event of an emergency, and extend the same offer to them. I recommend formalizing this type of arrangement and creating a two-way street before disaster strikes.

Moving the concentric circle further out may prove difficult for some of you. Not everyone lives near relatives and close friends. If this isn't a possibility, I suggest you make a list of hotels and campsites along your different "escape routes," and mark them on a map. Include phone numbers and addresses on the list, keeping this in your BOLT kit. The purpose of this secondary location is to get you far enough out of the fray to remain safe while keeping you connected to recovery efforts. You should have a list of several locations at varying distances from home to give you plenty of options based on the scope and severity of the disaster. As soon as you make the decision to leave, start making phone calls to secure shelter. Offer to pay in cash as an incentive to secure a reservation. Remember, you're not the only one that read a "prepping" book.

Beyond the second level of "bug out" readiness, we're starting to talk about more permanent relocation options. This is what I call the "the brother-in-law living in rural Vermont option." My wife's brother must be sweating our arrival at this point. Other options include that nice, overnight summer camp you sent your kids to for a week several years ago. The one on the secluded lake with a sturdy lodge and huge stone fireplace—that's empty nine months of the year. You might have to get creative with these locations if you don't have a brother-in-law a few states away. The one thing all of your "bug out" locations should have in common is long-term access to the SURVIVAL BASICS—food, water and shelter. You don't want to trade one problem for another.

I'll leave you with one final consideration. ***Whatever you do, make your decision early.*** When the county sheriff knocks on your door and points to a wall of smoke in the distance, you want to be one of the first families to leave the neighborhood. Fire doesn't stop or slow down for traffic. Have you ever seen the images of traffic leading out of Houston when Hurricane Rita hit on the heels of Hurricane Katrina? There's little point to sitting in a ten-lane traffic jam with a fully loaded car, trying to get out of dodge with everyone else. Having a solid escape plan in place beforehand can spell the difference between success and failure in a crisis.

Randall

The question posed in this chapter is the one that anyone practicing personal preparedness dreads most, yet it's the one that folks tend to spend the most time thinking about. Possibly even to the point of obsession, but maybe that's because they understand just how important a decision it really is. And there's so much to consider. Why would you ever leave your home, and when do you go? How would you leave, and what would you take with you? Where would you go, and what do you plan to do when you get there? Do you feel that twitch of panic creeping into your chest? Well, I haven't really scratched the surface of this topic yet. Get this call right and you may get out in front of the crowds and never really feel the danger and fear associated with the disaster. Make the wrong call and, depending on the situation, it could literally cost you your life. Without a doubt, this is the big one.

Bugging out or getting out of dodge, exactly what you call the process of evacuating doesn't really matter because it all means essentially the same thing. Something's gone down and you are forced to leave your home or primary shelter. Instead of a bug out bag (BOB) or a get out of dodge (GOOD) bag, we recommend you plan, build and maintain a BOLT (basic operations for a limited time) kit for just this situation that is built to fit your evacuation plan. If you need a refresher on the BOLT kit or philosophy, just flip back to chapter 16 for a moment. No rush, we'll wait.

Keep in mind, you don't have to wake up to the end of the world as we know it (TEOTWAWKI) before you may have to (or choose to) evacuate your home. The situation could be that you are facing a regional event or an emergency of limited duration and you will be able to eventually return home. Maybe you simply foresee an extended loss of power and decide to stay with family over a long weekend. With these instances in mind, we would urge you to consider what it really means to evacuate or *bug out* in today's world.

Although none of the reasons that might make us consider leaving our home could be considered a good time, they also certainly do not mean the world is coming to an end, and how you might deal with them doesn't have to make you feel that way either. As we've seen in recent years, even the most destructive and disruptive weather events, like the hurricanes Katrina and Sandy respectively, have been regional in scope. Their impacts, though devastating for local communities, have failed to rise to a national level. Situations like these allow you to survive and get through the event by taking advantage of the complex system of options still available to you outside the zone impacted by the event. A short ride to a friend's house a few miles away, a visit to a hotel a couple of hours from home, or dropping in at a family member's house for an extended visit might be just the ticket to a very successful bug out. Just make sure the plans are in place ahead of the disaster, especially if you're planning on staying with friends or family. See? You don't always have to grab your pack and trek off into the woods to possibly never be heard from again, and this way you can still have a comfortable bed to sleep in. This is how the majority of "real world" bug out scenarios actually play out. When given the option, people will overwhelmingly choose an option similar to those mentioned above, and why wouldn't they? Unless we're talking about an event on a national or global scale, these types of solutions are absolute winners, and what's more, you might even enjoy spending a little time with the in-laws.

So what's the plan should the towering clouds of disaster darken our door? Well, if you've picked up anything so far about how we do things, it will come as no surprise that planning and resilience play a key role in any possible evacuation scenario we may face. Depending on what's going on, we have a series of BOLT destinations that extend out from our home in concentric rings, offering multiple directional options where we could go should we be forced to leave. Both friends and family are represented in our BOLT destination options; everyone involved is aware of the plan and knows that our home is open to them for the same purpose should the need ever arise. Acknowledging that we may not always be able to remain at home during a disaster, we have built our BOLT kits to ensure not all will be lost should we ever have to activate our BOLT destination sites and evacuate. Having these plans in place, we face each day with confidence. We're not waiting for disaster to strike, but we know that if it does, we have done all we can to be able to ride out the wave in relative comfort and with peace of mind.

If you like how that sounds, just know you can do it too. All it takes is a little forethought, planning and communication. There's no time like the present, and if your friends and family are anything like mine, I know they would love to hear from you. So what are you waiting for? Reach out and link up today. Your safety and security during a disaster is only a phone call away.

PART 5: WHAT'S THE POINT?

Randall

As I write this, that old moon is rolling across the sky as another day draws to a close here in the United States in 2014. What an amazing time to be alive. Living in the most complex society the world has ever known certainly has its advantages. In about ten minutes, using nothing more than my smartphone and an internet connection, I can get up to speed with all of the news from around the globe while sitting in my pajamas in my living room. Take just a moment and let the brilliance of that reality wash over you. With access like that, it is certainly easy to keep your finger on the pulse of the world.

As a society we are drowning in information, and the news that is so easily and quickly delivered to us is not always good. You don't even have to be looking for them and you will find stories of war, economic troubles, or worse. The headlines of reality are right there to be read if we are willing to see them. To be certain, it is not difficult to find the motivation to take steps to be more prepared.

When we decided to take a more focused approach to preparedness a few years back, the one promise I made to Alice was that I would never let it take over my life or restrict our life together. Keep in mind that she is on board with everything we do, but we still wanted to make a concerted effort to keep things in perspective and within reason. We applied the practices and philosophies outlined in this book and attacked the problem. As a result of this approach, we have reached virtually all of our personal preparedness goals, yet we have still managed to do any and everything outside the world of preparedness we have wanted to do during that time. We still have careers we enjoy, watch our favorite sports, go to concerts and enjoy time with family and friends. When it comes to personal preparedness, you can absolutely have your cake and eat it too.

We believe that pursuing a preparedness lifestyle is a responsibility we have to each other as well as to our family and friends. Preparing gives you a feeling of independence knowing you are in a better position to take care of yourself and your family. Who among us would not do everything within our power to make certain our loved ones are safe and secure, especially if you were aware of some possible threat ahead of time? What's more, actively practicing personal preparedness is one of the most patriotic things you can do as a citizen. It is a statement declaring that you are an aware and independent citizen that understands the world around you and the responsibilities you bear in it. Think about it. If fewer people had to make that last minute run to the store to buy up food and supplies in an emergency, the just-in-time delivery system that our society depends upon might stand half a chance of surviving the initial surge of panicked shoppers. Every person that does not have to call for assistance from the emergency services takes pressure off of the system, possibly freeing up resources that can be used to help someone else. By preparing now, you become part of the solution by taking steps to remove yourself from the victim equation, thus potentially saving the lives of your fellow citizens. Now, how cool is that? Even if things don't play out that way, at the very least you are not placing even more strain on a system that will already be stretched thin during a disaster. Hopefully by having taken steps to prepare in advance, you will be in a better position to positively impact the emergency situation by helping your neighbors.

Think about the people in your life for a moment and remind yourself of why you're reading this book in the first place. That is what is important. It is those people and those relationships that will keep you going whenever the road looks long or the task seems too great. Believe in the process, and whatever level of preparedness you feel is appropriate, you can reach your goals.

Our preparedness journey continues, and we want to congratulate you on being brave enough to have started yours. The work of preparedness will never be finished, nor should it be. Personal circumstance and external situations are constantly evolving, and we must evolve with them. With this in mind, each of us can have a real impact on our personal situation by taking practical steps today to be more prepared. What started as a need to help myself turned into a desire to help others and has become a way of life. Our preparedness journey has proven to be a tremendous blessing in our lives. Not only are we ready to face down any of the most likely threats we have identified based on our situation, the process of preparing has added a richness, depth and beauty to our lives that we never would have expected. All of this and I've still managed to keep my promise to the most important person in my world. *That's what I'd call a win-win.*

The reality of our world is bad things happen to good people every day, and more often than not we are powerless to prevent them. None of us can know where disaster will strike next, but what we can do as rugged individuals is take steps right now to mitigate the impacts of the next disaster on our daily lives. Once you begin your journey to preparedness, we believe you will find that you are happier, more knowledgeable, and will develop a greater peace of mind.

We want to wish you the best of luck in your preparedness efforts. Just remember, you've already succeeded just by getting started!

The Practical Tactical Quick Start Guide is a fantastic nuts and bolts handbook outlining many of the concepts explored in this book. It's a great companion piece for quick reference.

Please visit Practical Tactical at PracticalTactical4you.com when you get a chance, we'd love to hear from you.

Steven

I very much doubt you're asking that question right now, but Randy and I thought this would be a fitting title to the last essay. We'll each go our own ways with the topic, but I suspect we'll end up in the same place at the end. Since Randy's essay will no doubt be far more informational and insightful, I'll take a different tack. I have something to admit that might surprise you. I immediately loved Randy's suggestion for the title, since I frequently ask myself, "What's the point?"

That's right. The author of *The Jakarta Pandemic, The Perseid Collapse* series and *Practical Prepping: No Apocalypse Required*, asks that question whenever he makes a bigger purchase or considers an equipment upgrade. Guess what? You will too.

Instinctively, we all know that the chances of an EMP attack or a disaster catapulting society into the Stone Age is HIGHLY unlikely. Zombies aren't real, contrary to what many believe, and pandemic-grade viruses, for all of their lethality throughout history, have rarely exceeded at two percent case fatality rate (2 out of 100 people that contract the disease dies). We've seen examples of frightening television coverage of civil disturbances in recent U.S history, but the rioting rarely lasts longer than a week, and is almost always contained to a specific geographic area. Big earthquakes hit the West Coast, right? I just did a quick Internet search. Not to minimize the rest of the earthquakes, but the last truly devastating earthquake occurred in 1906, killing over three thousand people. Hurricanes strike every year, but who remembers any of the hurricanes between Katrina and Sandy? What about a tsunami? Once again, I can think of two tsunamis in my lifetime. Let's face it, planning for the Big Kahuna scenario can seem like overkill.

But so does carrying more than the absolute minimum required car insurance, showing up for your annual physical exam (when you're twenty-five), paying term life insurance premiums until you're sixty-five, locking your car doors at the supermarket, checking your windows and doors right before you go to bed, walking your kid to the bus stop at the end of your street, changing your online banking password, carrying a concealed weapon into public—*we routinely safeguard ourselves and our loved ones against the most UNLIKELY problems, at great cost and inconvenience!*

I'm not saying you need to prepare for the apocalypse. We added NO APOCALYPSE REQUIRED to our title for a reason. Randy and I fully embrace the need to strike a balance between living a preparedness lifestyle and "living your life." If anything, my approach falls A LOT further along the "living your life" side of the spectrum than the other. Having taken this balanced approach, my family is ready for our most likely SURVIVE WHAT scenario, and we're taking slow, steady strides toward preparing for a bigger crisis. *That's all I could ever ask of my family, friends, neighbors, and readers.*

I wish you all success in your readiness journey!

If you haven't read my novels, you can check out my post-apocalyptic titles at StevenKonkoly.com: *The Jakarta Pandemic*, *The Perseid Collapse (Book 1 in The Perseid Collapse Series)*, *Event Horizon (Book 2 in The Perseid Collapse Series)*, *Point of Crisis* (Book 3 in The Perseid Collapse Series)

Please visit StevenKonkoly.com to learn more about current and future projects.

The author welcomes any comments, feedback or questions at:

stevekonkoly@gmail.com

Pandemic Primer

I finished writing my essays for Practical Prepping before the Ebola outbreak made international headlines in July 2014. Since then, I've received numerous requests for my opinion on the situation, and how to prepare for a similar outbreak in the United States. First, I want to put the current Ebola outbreak into perspective. Worldwide, seasonal flu strains kill anywhere between 250,000 to 500,000 people annually. Seasonal flu is the highly contagious influenza that typically hits us in the fall, lasting throughout the spring. In the United States, rough estimates place the number of season flu related deaths between 30,000 to 40,000, with no fewer than several hundred deaths recorded per week during peak flu season (CDC data)—Jan thru April. Even in the miserable conditions of western-central Africa, only 1,145 suspected case deaths have been recorded (as of August 18, 2014) since detection in March 2014. Frankly, you probably have a better chance of dying from season flu on your vacation to Monrovia than Ebola. ***I still recommend putting a hold on any exotic travel plans to Africa.***

Am I worried about the Ebola virus becoming the next great pandemic? Not really. The low case death rates are attributed to Ebola's method of transmission. Unlike seasonal flu or pandemic grade influenza viruses (Swine and Avian Flu), Ebola is not easily spread through the air or on surfaces like influenza. Currently, Ebola is transmitted through direct contact with the blood or bodily fluids of infected patients. Another factor slowing Ebola is its calculated generation time, or time to infect another person. Seasonal influenza has a generation time of 2-4 days, while Ebola takes 14-21 days. Both of these factors conspire to keep Ebola from spreading rapidly, as evidenced in Africa.

The problem with Ebola is its confirmed lethality. Case fatality rates (percentage of those infected that die) historically range anywhere from 25-90%, with the latest strain of Zaire strain hovering toward the high end of that spectrum. In contrast, historical pandemic flu viruses have rarely exceeded a 2% case fatality rate. *Scary to say the least.* Since there's no vaccine or unique treatment to handle patients, Ebola has traditionally been considered a likely death sentence—and a nasty one at that. "Bleeding out" internally and externally is a horrific death.

Do you feel better about the Ebola virus now? You should. Public health experts (which we should all trust—can I quote Alex Fletcher on that?) agree that a virus like Ebola would have little chance of spreading in a developed country with a robust healthcare infrastructure. Complain all you like about the high cost of healthcare and long wait times in your doctor's office, but the U.S. has one of the best healthcare infrastructures in the world.

I'd spend a less time worrying about the Ebola virus and more time preparing for the inevitable pandemic flu virus. Avian Flu is a hop, skip and a jump away from mutating into a strain capable of efficient human-to-human transmission, and unlike Ebola, strains of Avian influenza have all of the characteristics needed for a quick spread across a developed nation like the United States. Using modern transportation, a pandemic grade flu virus could spread from coast to coast in a matter of hours, rendering containment efforts nearly impossible. Epidemiologists estimate that the Spanish Flu of 1918 infected 500 million of the world's 1.8 billion people, killing 50-100 million of them. Considering the modes of transportation available in 1918, I think it's fair to say that every person in every corner of the globe will be threatened by the next great pandemic. What can you do to better your odds of survival? Funny you should ask.

I've said it before, and I'll say it again. Strict quarantine is the only way to guarantee that you won't get infected. I know, easier said than done. On top of that, you need to know when it's time to initiate quarantine. Hint: BEFORE THE FLU ARRIVES IN YOUR COMMUNITY. You're probably wondering why you paid for this advice. Hang in there.

Early or timely detection is the key to avoiding exposure. This means picking the right time to 1. Pull the kids out of school—they're sick with flu symptoms! 2. Take a few weeks of unplanned vacation (death in the family is a great excuse—don't judge, it may save your life). 3. Start gathering everyone in your survival group—no point in having infected people showing up a week into the pandemic. 4. Make those last minute preparedness purchases before everyone is sneezing in line at the grocery store.

How will you know when it's time? Ideally, you would be friends with the director of your local hospital's infectious disease department (like Alex Fletcher in The Jakarta Pandemic). If not, you should pay attention to reports of pandemic grade viral outbreaks in major cities around the globe or in your country. It's not common for Avian Flu or Swine Flu to show up outside of very specific areas in the world. Swine Flu (H1N1) can be found anywhere in the world. In 2009 it reared its ugly head in Mexico and quickly spread worldwide. Avian Flu (H5N1) is typically found in southeast Asia (China, Vietnam). *When you start seeing reports of Avian Flu in London, Munich and Moscow, it might be time to get your affairs in order.* I watch the following websites closely for the latest breaking outbreak news, along with the CDC and WHO websites.

www.cidrap.umn.edu – Center for Infectious Disease Research and Policy. Great collation of latest updates

www.outbreaks.globalincidentmap.com/home.php – This may look familiar for readers of The Jakarta Pandemic

Once you've determined that the next great pandemic is coming, it's time to get serious, but remain realistic. The Jakarta Pandemic represented the "perfect storm" in that I unleashed an exceptionally lethal and contagious flu at the worst time of the year in New England. I also enhanced the characteristics of H16N1 to be the perfect killing machine under those circumstances. In reality, we will likely face a much less virulent flu strain, which is unlikely to catapult society into chaos for months. Unless you're hit with a major storm during the most intense period of the first or second wave of the pandemic, you're unlikely to lose power, and only then if it's a massive pandemic. I'll slap my SURVIVE WHAT card on the table and say you need plan on becoming SELF SUFFICIENT and SELF CONTAINED—QUARANTINED for at least 2-4 weeks during each wave of the pandemic.

What do I mean by waves? Pandemic flus strike in several waves (3-4), usually 2 to 3 months apart, with the second wave typically measured as the most lethal. Surviving the first wave in quarantine means you'll be at high risk for the second wave, unless a vaccine is administered before the second wave arrives. If the virus is a new strain, a vaccine will not be ready in time for the second wave. I recommend that you be ready for a second period of self-sufficient isolation.

Unlike seasonal flu strains, which follow a relatively stable pattern of emergence (late fall-depending on your hemisphere), pandemic flus can emerge at any time. Depending on your location, overall planning for a 2-4 week quarantine period will vary. While I won't go into regional recommendations for shelter, heat, food and power in this primer, I will make some pandemic specific recommendations.

Actions to Consider:

-Use up vacation time or request an emergency leave of absence when you determine that a pandemic grade virus is inbound. Once your co-workers are coughing and sniffling, it's too late.

-Take your kids out of school early. We all know how quickly disease spreads through a school.

-Avoid public areas, unless absolutely necessary—and only then wearing the proper personal protective gear (explained later).

-Fill cars with gas for unexpected travel, and keep extra gas on hand to run your generator.

-Order your fireplace wood, if you haven't already. Especially important for colder parts of the country.

-Get cash. You can always put it back.

-Gather members of your survival team. Quarantine means quarantine. Uncle Eddie shouldn't roll into town hacking and dripping snot after you've locked the doors. Be as proactive as possible managing this aspect of your plan.

Supplies to Consider:

-N95, surgical grade masks in case you have to the leave the house.

-Sterile gloves plus hand sanitizer. The hands spread most of the disease.

-Disinfectant agent. Don't mess around here. The easiest disinfectant to create and administer is a bleach solution. Buy a few empty spray bottles and create your own solution. Add 1 tablespoon of bleach to 1 quart (4 cups) of water. For a larger supply of disinfectant, add ¼ cup of bleach to 1 gallon (16 cups) of water. Keep this handy to spray down surfaces suspected of infection.

-Stored water. I keep at least 40 gallons on hand at any time, in 2.5 gallon containers (the one with the spigot).

-Water purification tablets or a water purifier. You are unlikely to lose water in a pandemic, but the chance exists if the power goes out for an extended period.

-Food for 2-4 weeks—let's just say 4 weeks and call it good! 4 weeks is my magic number for any home stockpile.

-First aid kit, expanded to including fever and cold medicine. You don't want to venture out for basic medical needs once the pandemic is in full effect.

-Vitamins to boost immunity. Consider naturopathic sources like Oreganoil or Elderberry syrup—don't laugh! We use this all winter and RARELY get more than the most basic, one-day cold. Fair warning—this stuff is expensive.

-Toilet paper and trash bags.

-Hand cranked radio (I always recommend this)

-Candles

-Propane stove for basic cooking plus propane canisters.

As you can see, the actions are basic, and most of the supplies I recommend can be "cannibalized" from your established SURVIVE WHAT scenario. You'll probably need to order sterile gloves, N95 masks, vitamins and bleach. In the interest of full disclosure, I'll admit that I just now ordered masks and gloves. Yes, the author of The Jakarta Pandemic has been sitting around with no sterile gloves and masks for about a year now. I'm not totally to blame! My daughter loves to play "doctor" with the gloves and masks. There's only so much I can do around here to stay on top of things!

Keep in mind that I've described a basic level of preparation. The most important aspects of a Pandemic plan are 1.) EARLY DETECTION and 2.) SELF SUFFICIENT, SELF CONTAINED living for at leat 4 weeks. Yes, I just eliminated the 2-week option. The lawyers told me to err on the side of caution. Occasionally they give good advice.

If you want to go deep into this topic, I recommend that you read The Jakarta Pandemic. Normally, I'm really shy about plugging my own books, but the amount of research distilled into The Jakarta Pandemic filled several binders and spanned nearly a month of intense reading. You won't regret it, and "it might save your life." I didn't say that originally—an Amazon reviewer said it.

As always, if you have questions or concerns about pandemic preparedness, please don't hesitate to contact me at skpandemic@gmail.com. No emergency questions please! I sometimes take a few days to respond, and by then it might be too late. Cue the scary music.

Resources

Websites – type into Google the keywords below (to access)

Other than our own, we like:

The Survival Mom: Geared toward "moms," valuable for EVERYONE.

SurvivalBlog.com: No list is complete without James Wesley Rawles' comprehensive site. If you can't find it here, it doesn't exist.

Backdoor Survival: Easy to grasp, home-style approach to prepping. Not planning on building a bomb shelter? This is your place.

Survivalist Boards: Forum based prepare/survivalist community. Ask a question, get detailed, comprehensive answers.

When SHTF: Forum based community. This is the first place I submitted The Jakarta Pandemic for feedback.

Books

Randy likes:

The Encyclopedia of Country Living, 10th Edition by Carla Emery

When Technology Fails: A Manual for Self-Reliance, Sustainability, and Surviving the Long Emergency, 2nd Edition by Matthew Stein

Just in Case: How to Be Self-Sufficient When the Unexpected Happens by Kathy Harrison and Alison Kolesar

The Crash Course: The Unsustainable Future Of Our Economy, Energy, And Environment by Chris Martenson

Steven likes:

Anything that Randy likes...plus

The SAS Survival Handbook by John Wiseman

Survival Field Manual FM 21-76 Department of the Army (easy to find)

The Backyard Homestead by Carleen Madigan

The Urban Homestead by Kelly Coyne and Erik Knutzen